SOUMITRA CHATTERJEE

Soumitra Chatterjee with his mother, Ashalata Devi

Photo courtesy of Partha Mukherjee

SOUMITRA CHATTERJEE

A Life in Cinema, Theatre, Poetry & Painting

ARJUN SENGUPTA

&

PARTHA MUKHERJEE

NIYOGI
BOOKS

Published by
NIYOGI BOOKS
Block D, Building No. 77,
Okhla Industrial Area, Phase-I,
New Delhi-110 020, INDIA
Tel: 91-11-26816301, 26818960
Email: niyogibooks@gmail.com
Website: www.niyogibooksindia.com

Editor: Sucharita Ghosh
Design: Shashi Bhushan Prasad

ISBN: 978-93-89136-76-0
Publication: 2020

The views and opinions expressed in the book are purely in the personal capacity of the authors and do not reflect the views of any official positions that they may hold.

Printed at: Niyogi Offset Pvt. Ltd., New Delhi, India

CONTENTS

Photo courtesy of Pratap Dasgupta

INTRODUCTION

In *Apur Sansar*, the last film of Satyajit Ray's masterful Apu trilogy, we are introduced to the protagonist as a young man. Ray had built Apu with meticulous care in the first two films (*Pather Panchali* and *Aparajito*), capturing his journey from boyhood to adolescence through a precise, insightful script and intuitive flashes of cinematic poetry. *Aparajito* ends with death and Apu on the cusp of manhood. In *Apur Sansar*, he takes his final step towards maturity and wisdom.

In the first scene of the film, Apu tells his teacher that he has no money to continue his education. Apu, played by a young man in his first film, is youthful and sensitive looking, his winsome smile masking his apprehensions about the future. His teacher is visibly disappointed, and before he leads him out into a world of unrest and strife right outside the door, he implores him to keep writing.

Apu pauses, and then walks out. Looking back, it is a scene that is so much more than just about the character in the film. At that point the actor playing Apu, Soumitra Chatterjee, is also about to embark on a journey – a journey that in terms of longevity and sustained excellence alone has ensured his place in the pantheon of the greatest actors ever produced in India. He has been Satyajit Ray's 'one-man stock company' (according to Pauline Kael), a superstar at the box office, an actor of such versatility and craft that he's worked with almost all the major directors of Bengali cinema of his time, a distinguished character actor, an equally accomplished actor on stage, poet, playwright and painter. He has worked with Satyajit Ray in fourteen films, a partnership that can only be effectively compared to the ones between Akira Kurosawa and Toshiro Mifune, and Martin Scorsese and Robert De Niro in world cinema.

It has been sixty years since the release of *Apur Sansar*. A long and very illustrious career has followed this first moment of triumph. Soumitra's office is in a small neatly arranged adjunct to a white, largely non-descript bungalow tucked away in a corner of Golf Green in Kolkata. If you do not have an appointment, you will be politely but firmly stopped by a burly guard near the gate. Once he has confirmed that you are not a gatecrasher trying your luck, you are escorted into his office. There is nothing forbidding about the house. There are no high walls or very tight security anywhere. Soumitra is one of the most easily recognisable figures in Bengal, but you would not know it by simply looking around. Soumitra tenaciously maintains his identity as an educated *bhadrolok* and, so far as that goes, any overt display of his fame would be distasteful in the extreme.

You can get a little lost finding his house, at which point you should make your way to the nearest rickshaw stand and get your bearings. You will get very precise directions there, and chances are one of them will add: 'You really just have to say his name. Anyone here will show you his house.'

He is right, of course. Everyone knows his place.

Despite the apparent normality of the surroundings, it is nevertheless a little nerve-wracking to meet him for the first time. A rather life-like portrait of him as he is now is propped up on the divan. It smiles at all visitors with generous exuberance. The room is a little bare apart from that.

When he walks in and greets you, the nervousness gives way to a slight dissonance, like you have just come a little unstuck in time. It is difficult to not see all the celluloid versions of him jostling for attention in one's memory marching in together with him and conflating themselves with the real person. He probably knows it too, and so he will put you at ease. There are no pictures of him as a younger man anywhere. It is not really surprising when you get to know him a little better.

He is always looking ahead – to the next project, the next film, the next production. He does not have much use for the laurels that have multiplied prodigiously in the course of his life. He is content to have let time had its say. The contours of his easily recognisable features have shifted over the years, and while they have gained in urbane gentility, there is still the curiosity of a small boy in his intelligent eyes. He smiles easily and, when he does, images from a career spanning six decades flash by like the projections of a zoetrope marking the evolution of Bengali cinema itself.

For generations of Bengali children, their earliest and most abiding memories of him are as Feluda in *Sonar Kella* and *Joy Baba Felunath*. He is always happy when you bring that up and says: 'Do you know how many people have said this to me? Ever since the early 1980s. Now their children and grandchildren say that to me!'

There is no doubting that. Growing up in a time when there were no more than a couple of channels on TV, and when the largely commercial fare of regional and national cinema were the not-too-subtle actioners, reruns of Feluda gave us a hero who was cerebral, and for whom physical violence was always the last distasteful resort. And even though much has changed in post-liberalisation India, Feluda remains a cultural mainstay in almost every Bengali household. It holds on with nimble tenacity even as it transitions gracefully into becoming an artefact of a previous era.

Soumitra has said in several interviews that while everyone thought Ray had modelled Feluda on him, he always thought that he was really a fictional version of Ray himself. It is not hard to believe. The detective's quiet intensity, encyclopaedic knowledge and keen intelligence are as much a projection of the author's own character as they are a homage to his archetypal ancestor at 221B Baker Street.

'I had a lot of fun shooting those films, especially *Joy Baba Felunath* because of the setting. I remember sitting on the steps of the ghat and saying that either I will take revenge for this or I'll give up being a detective.'

It is a favourite dialogue of his and he mentions it in many of his interviews. He can still slip easily into character whenever he says it and for an instant

Soumitra in conversation with actor Naseeruddin Shah
Photo courtesy of Supriyo Nag

he is Feluda again. It is very difficult to not fanboy all over him when he does. Nostalgia is a powerful thing and his Feluda is an inextricable part of it – associated with our best childhood memories.

The enduring popularity of Feluda is in no small measure due to him. While several actors have tried to put their best foot forward with the character, their portrayals are haunted by his performance – as if his Feluda was a real person and everyone else's portrayal must necessarily fall short of the real thing. He does not believe that though. He is happy that the character continues to be popular even after all these years.

It has however ensured his continuing survival as a pop culture icon. The books and the character, now inseparable from his performance, have become over the years important enough to almost be a rite of passage for a Bengali growing up. The books, with Ray's illustrations bearing an uncanny

Photo courtesy of Supriyo Nag

resemblance with the actor, peek out of bookshelves in millions of households. And then there are the films, the enormous appeal of which no number of viewings can abate or diminish. In a career studded with all the accolades it is possible for an actor who never ventured out of regional cinema to get, Soumitra has been awarded them all. Yet it is his hawk-eyed, well mannered, intellectually gifted detective with a profound sense of right and wrong that will always have the widest universal appeal.

There is a bit of a paradox in this though, and he is not unaware of it. Actors who achieve a certain stature invariably have to deal with their widely accepted public personas. They become like doppelgängers mediating between the individual and the public at large. Cary Grant had once famously said that everyone wants to be Cary Grant, and that even he too would like to be Cary Grant.

Soumitra Chatterjee, as far as public perception goes, has over the years become less an individual and more an iconic emblem symbolising by turns the different aspects of Bengali culture with which he is associated. He is now the lone survivor of a golden generation. While he wears the mantle easily, he is not exactly the most typical person you would expect in that position.

He is broadly regarded as one of the most gifted actors in the country but that does not alone define his place in Bengali cinema. He was second only to the legendary Uttam Kumar at the box office, which in the circumstances was a monumental feat in itself. It also meant that he was a major star, a performer who could ensure commercial returns by his presence alone. In spite of this, he never actively vied for any of the trappings of stardom. He has been asked countless times about the superstardom of Uttam Kumar and what he thought about their rivalry. He is always very patient in his declarations of admiration for the megastar.

'There was no one to touch him. But I feel that he was very protective of his stardom. He did his talents injustice because he didn't want to experiment too much.'

He does not feel diminished by comparisons though. He is quick to add that the era was defined not by Uttam Kumar alone but by Uttam and Soumitra. He is pretty clear about it too. Does he regret not paying greater heed to the demands of stardom? He shakes his head and says that he was determined to do as wide a repertoire of roles as possible. In short, he wanted to be true to his vocation. If there is a continuing conflict, some residual longing for the road not taken, it is not apparent at all. He has managed to actively keep the allure of stardom at bay all his life.

He will smile and tell you that there was no real conflict to begin with. 'You see, there can have been no conflict. It would have ruined everything. I knew that what I wanted most of all was to act in roles that challenged me. I had taken my decision, and never had cause to regret it.'

It cannot have been an easy decision. As an artist, Soumitra has been keenly protective of his artistic integrity. He lends his voice and face to advertisements of various kinds, and one would be hard-pressed to travel very far in and around Kolkata without finding him smiling down benignly from a billboard. This may seem like a contradiction but it does not bother him. It has nothing to do with his credentials as an artist, but a simple case of leveraging the aforementioned public persona for commercial ends.

He is the kind of person who has always searched for the right reasons to do what he has achieved in his career. When he looks back upon his life to discern some wellspring of motivation that, while invisible at the time, played a role in all the decisions he took, he finds a governing ambition amidst all the minutiae of a long and varied career. He is after all not just an actor of the cinema and the theatre. He is an accomplished writer, poet, and artist among other things. If his inherent creative urges branched out in these directions like streams from a river, what determined their direction and course?

'I suppose it all had to have some purpose.'

As a young man, Soumitra did not have the greatest regard for cinema. He was an ardent student of the legendary thespian Sisir Kumar Bhaduri and, if not for the intervention of Ray, he may not have stepped too far out of the proscenium arch. He needed greater moral or artistic justifications for his choice of career and, indeed, for the decisions he took all through his life. It had to do as much with the manner in which he had been brought up, as it had to do with the fact that he was a widely read, ethically conscious individual for whom art could never simply be an end in itself.

'It was not just acting. I really wanted to give something back to society, do something important and constructive.'

He would not have it any other way.

Photo courtesy of Pratap Dasgupta

SOUMITRA – THE MAN

Soumitra Chatterjee has been so many things and has played so many roles in his long career that to pin him down and look for an easy definition can only be counter-productive. And perhaps pointless! Actors are complicated people, oddly conflicted as only people whose profession is to pretend to be other people can be. Moreover, Soumitra has always chafed at being pigeonholed in any strict category. He never settled into a comfortable groove as an actor, and refused to let acting come in the way of his other pursuits. In fact, sixty years into a celebrated career on screen, he is now enthused most about his projects in theatre, his poetry and his painting. Soumitra has always been a private person, even though paradoxically enough, he can be very outspoken and frank when he wants to. He can be the quintessentially refined and well-educated intellectual, or he will caustically tell you that there have been few people in the industry as foul-mouthed as him. It is possible that he switches through personas from his repertoire in real life like a skilled actor can from role to role. It is more probable that they are different facets of a complex nature.

Soumitra has written and spoken at length about his views on not just his craft, but on all the varied subjects that he is passionate about. Sometimes, there are glimpses into his personal life, but they are elusive and always aware of the fine line between what is private and what is fit for public consumption. He is a careful man that way, but it also has to do with deep-rooted insecurities that go back a long way to his childhood. He says that as an actor he is used to expressing himself through different personas and voices. He has always found it difficult to speak about his own experiences in his own voice. In this, he is not unusual. An actor has to contend with the fact that everyone knows not him but the roles he has played. There are many celebrated cases of actors who have never quite come to terms with this.

He had a happy childhood in Krishnanagar, but there were unexpected anxieties. He remembers how his relatives did not think much about the way he looked. There are pictures of him that are less than flattering. He grew up thinking that he was not particularly good-looking. This made him self-conscious which he tried to cover up with a lively boisterousness. It hid a sensitivity that made it difficult for him to express his true self to the world.

His family was involved with the local theatre scene and he started acting in the natural course of things. It would become a proper vocation much later in Calcutta under the tutelage of Sisir Kumar Bhaduri. Yet even in his boyhood forays he won praise and a fair bit of local renown. This became a very liberating experience for him, allowing him to mask his insecurities by freely becoming someone else. This preference for a mask or person as a mediator between his intensely shy self and the public at large has continued for the rest of his life. Even decades later, he still does not believe in autobiographies. He doubts whether anyone would want to know anything about his life, or even whether it is possible to really encapsulate a person in his complicated totality in a book. Above all, he wonders whether it would matter. He would rather be known by his work. Yet the unusual trajectory of his career and his choices as an artist have perhaps revealed more about the kind of person he is than a full-length expository tract on his personal life could ever have.

It is not as if he wants his life to be shrouded in mystery. If you ask anyone who has interviewed him over the years, they will tell you that he can be quite forthcoming. His passionate nature can quite often be fiery. He has no qualms about telling you about the time he punched Ritwik Ghatak in the face. Apparently, it was during the turbulent years in the late 1970s when the industry was going through a crisis, and there was a meeting called between all the stakeholders to resolve the issue. Soumitra says Ritwik who had a foul mouth was keeping up a steady stream of insults directed at Satyajit Ray who was not present. Soumitra understood that he was trying to rile him up. It was definitely annoying but he did not respond because he did not think someone like Ray needed anyone to defend him. Eventually Ritwik, failing to draw blood with his taunts at Ray, directed a few snarky comments at Soumitra who refused to take it lying down. He caught him by the collar, felled him with a punch and told him off in no uncertain terms – 'You're not dealing with a mild-mannered *bhadrolok* here,' he remembers saying.

However, this has never stopped him from freely acknowledging Ritwik's massive talent. He regrets never having had the opportunity to work with him. He had come very close, and was even supposed to meet him, but Ritwik turned up very late and drunk. Soumitra did not like that. He had been schooled in the hard school of professionalism by Ray, and he was not likely to make any exceptions for anybody.

Yet when it came to his mentors, Sisir Kumar and Ray, he was always the attentive and humble student. In fact, it is his dedicated loyalty to his mentors that is perhaps the most representative feature of his character. He is the quintessential company man, if by company one means the people he looked up to for intellectual and artistic guidance. He has written at length about the various technical accomplishments of Sisir Kumar as an actor and his massive contribution to Bengali theatre. He tirelessly defends him against what he thinks is ignorant or misplaced criticism. He met Sisir Kumar when the legend was at the end of his career. There was a significant difference between their ages. There was not enough time for them to forge a long and intimate relationship. Sisir Kumar remained a distant god he adored and from whom he learnt the foundations of his craft.

He is perhaps too close to the works of Ray (having acted in most of his films) to write about him in the same manner but in his *The Master and I*, he has written fondly about his time spent with the master. The fact that Ray acted the role of a surrogate parent in his life is probably a pretty easy deduction to make. Ray chose him, moulded him, and set him off upon his career. He was a paternal figure responsible for the beginning of his new life as a film

Soumitra receiving the Chevalier de la Légion d'honneur
(Chevalier of Legion of Honor) from the French Ambassador in 2018
Photo courtesy of Supriyo Nag

(Right to left) Soumitra with poet, lyricist and filmmaker Gulzar and writer Sunil Gangopadhyay
Photo courtesy of Pratap Dasgupta

actor. Furthermore, he kept a watchful eye on him all his life. Soumitra ascribes everything he knows about films to him. Even when he resumed theatre in earnest, Ray was there with his honest and helpful critiques. And like a true father figure, he would take him to task as well. Once when they were shooting *Devi*, Ray in an irritable mood discovered that Soumitra had not brought his dialogue sheets from the hotel. The location was more than a mile from the hotel, and Soumitra had already gone through costume and make-up. Ray peremptorily told him to go and get it. Humiliation comes easy to a young man, and Soumitra felt both hurt and angry. It was a knock on the head and as he later realised, a manifestation of Ray's fondness for him too. Ray's influence over the actor went beyond films, and he eventually became his guide in all matters of life, big and small. He was his family in a way no one in the industry has ever been. This is more than apparent in the manner he writes about him.

Soumitra is forthcoming with his opinions about most things, including his passion for sports as well as his political leanings. The former led to one of the best performances in his career in *Kony*, while the latter has been more difficult to sustain in disillusioning times. He was born in a very political time, when the country was still trying to figure out what to do with its hard-fought independence. There was excitement, hope and sometimes disillusionment. In Calcutta, caught in the welter of impassioned opinions, Soumitra aligned himself with a popular ideology so very attractive to idealistic students everywhere. Except, he did it with the same intense dedication he reserved for the most important things in his life. Even as an octogenarian, he quotes from the *Communist Manifesto* with ease – 'The history of all hitherto existing society is the history of class struggles.' In the years since the heady days of his youth, history has muddied the clear, egalitarian message of communism, and he has little hope for its future now. It has however become something akin to a creed for him, a catechism with which to deal with life in place of traditional religious beliefs. By his own admission, he finds more solace in it than he would have in religion. He never took that leap of faith that religion requires, but his internalisation of the 'spectre of communism' has held him in good stead.

He is not shy about how proud he is of his children either. He met his wife, Deepa, when he was only sixteen, and he speaks of her as the only true love of his life. She was an accomplished badminton player, a university blue. Soumitra is rather proud of that. He says that despite his great passion for sports he was not very good at it, and so it gave him great pleasure to have married someone who was. He married her ten years later in 1960. They had two children, a son and a daughter. He writes about their accomplishments with all the fondness of a doting father. His son Saugata was a very skilled violinist. When he was looking to buy his son an instrument from abroad, Ray had gifted him his grandfather's violin. Soumitra also made sure that his children had a firm grounding in Bengali, a natural fluency in which had first recommended him to Ray when he was searching for a young man to play the protagonist in *Apur Sansar*. Saugata has inherited this natural affinity for the language as well, and wrote very good poetry according to his father.

Characteristically enough, he kept his fame as a public figure quite separate from his personal life. He went out of his way to spend as much time as he could with his children. His daughter, Poulami, who has followed her father into the theatre recalls that he was always nothing more than 'Bapi' for them. This led to some rather amusing incidents. Poulami never understood why her father was a big deal. She would insist that he took her to school and be there to pick her up at the end of the day. Soumitra, who could not say no to her, would quite often have to take a break from a hectic shooting schedule to accommodate her demand. She got miffed sometimes when she saw her friends line up to get a glimpse of her father. 'I don't wait around to see any of your fathers,' she would say!

Once she needed supplies for a project at school and Soumitra took her to New Market. As word spread of his arrival, a small crowd began to form behind him. A passing spectator there would have seen a strange sight – a small girl leading a grown man carrying sundry packets fit to burst and at a respectful distance an admiring and pointing crowd. And then there was the time when they had gone on a vacation and found themselves on a Hindi film set. She was star-struck when Dharmendra came to talk to them, and even more surprised when she realised that the Bollywood superstar knew her father.

As she grew older, she understood more of her father's fame. He remained a devoted father helping her through the difficult teenage years by taking her out for *bhutta,* baked corn, by the riverside and letting her talk it out while he listened quietly. On Sundays, he took his children to Coffee House or to a friend's house. They would all look forward to the Sunday when they would go to Manik jethu's (Satyajit Ray) house, who in spite of his forbidding demeanour had a very special way with children. When Poulami wanted to become an actor, Soumitra asked Utpal Dutt to show her the ropes. This eventually led to a number of successful father-daughter collaborations.

It is a happy picture but it has not been an easy journey. He never wanted his family to be any different than the one he had grown up in, but that is not always compatible with a life of celebrity. The fact that there should be

Soumitra receiving the Padma Bhushan Award from The Honourable President of India A.P.J. Abdul Kalam in 2004
Photo courtesy of PTI

temptations in the life of a famous actor is a truism bordering on cliché, but it is still one of the pitfalls of a life of fame. In interviews, he regrets his indiscretions that have brought him and his family nothing but pain, and he admits that he could have been stronger.

He has also had his fair share of what he calls the 'cruelties of life'. His son's promising career as a virtuoso violinist was cut short because of a serious illness during his college days. He was himself diagnosed with cancer in 2010, and went through a period of severe anguish and fear. It is not surprising that he has tried to filter this fear into something meaningful through art. In his semi-autobiographical play *Tritiyo Onko Otoeb*, he faces his own mortality and

Soumitra receiving the Dadasaheb Phalke Award from The Honourable Vice President of India Mohammad Hamid Ansari in 2012
Photo courtesy of PTI

arrives at a semblance of acceptance of it. However, the greatest tragedy of his life that has cast a pall of gloom in his later years has been his grandson Ronodeep's (Poulami's son) near fatal accident in 2017. He has since been waging a grim battle against very difficult odds.

He still fights on, even though the struggle is becoming more and more difficult. He has not only lived through the greatest years of Bengali cinema, but was prominently responsible for them. He was the favoured actor of one of the greatest directors in the world, and still continues to turn out award-winning performances in films that are mediocre. It is difficult to not be trapped in the mausoleum of memories and stay hidden to spite a world that had changed for the worse. He had always looked up to his mentors for guidance, and now when they are all gone, he has nothing but an innate enthusiasm for the artist's life to fall back upon.

He has been awarded the Padma Bhushan and the Dadasaheb Phalke Award. He is also the recipient of the prestigious Légion d'honneur bestowed by the French government. But these honours probably redound more on the awards that they do on the recipient. In any case, he has never been one for awards, because he knows that in most cases, they have nothing to do with the craft of the artist. Besides, in a life spent running away from hollow accolades, he is the last person who needs the validation of awards. He would rather have a great role to play, because in a life that has not always been kind to him, he has nevertheless got the opportunity to play the most interesting characters ever put on film.

If he is not as famous outside Bengal as he should be, it has to do with his clear-minded understanding of what was best for him. After all, even Uttam Kumar was not proof to the lure of Bollywood. He was cast in Shyam Benegal's *Kalyug*, and he had even gone to Bombay to start shooting. It did not work out because he was never really comfortable in a setup that seemed alien to him. He always thought that his performance gained a lot of credibility from his proficiency in the Bengali language. He wondered if it would be the same in a language in which he was not fluent. He eventually left the production amicably, and Benegal cast Shashi Kapoor to play the role.

Soumitra's loyalty to his Bengali identity determined many of his decisions in his career. It turned out to be a wise choice because with the help of Ray and others, he managed to stay close to his roots while turning out performances of universal relevance. He has worked in Bengali cinema but in his legacy he belongs to world cinema. He has said in numerous interviews that he chose to use acting as a medium to do something of social significance. It is not surprising that a fervent communist would claim ideological motives behind his decisions. Truth be told, there were a number of reasons, including the peculiar circumstances of his own upbringing and the sociological significance of that instant in the history of Bengali cinema when he made his debut that has charted the course of his unique career.

As he grows older the weight of his achievements can often be a painful and frustrating burden. The blessings of a long, successful career are countered by a nagging feeling that the world may have changed a little too much. He has felt unmoored as his familiar world has slowly given way to spasmodic shifts in identity in a post-globalisation Bengal. It is probably why he feels that he is no longer as ambitious an actor as he used to be. The hunger is no longer there, he says. It is a poignant admission, especially coming from someone who has dedicated his life to perfecting his craft. It may well be a defense mechanism too. It is better to lose your passion than see your craft lose its edge unburnished in a lesser age. His performances now have all the relaxed ease of a professional who knows what is expected of him, and can deliver without putting too much of a strain on himself. It is however the strain that he misses the most, the leap into the unknown and do something no one thought he could. In his career, these chances have led to a startlingly diverse filmography.

He has no intention of giving up though. It would be something like admitting defeat, and a lifetime's worth of straining ahead in spite of risks is too much a part of his character for that. He keeps working in part to cock a defiant snook at his own frustrations, and because he does not know what he would do with his time. He says that he would have probably been a carpenter if he had not been an actor. It sounds flippant but his admiration for the craft of carpentry is genuine. It reveals something important about him too. He believes in creativity that is useful, something that will actually be helpful to people. He is still waiting for his next challenging role, another Gangacharan or Narsingh! Until then, when things get a little too bleak for him, he goads himself on to keep fighting, like Khit da from *Kony* – 'Fight, Kony, fight!'

Photo courtesy of Pratap Dasgupta

A HAPPY CHILDHOOD

Soumitra believes that he was always an actor in preparation, even though he knows that he did not do it consciously. He remembers growing up in Krishnanagar, Darjeeling, and eventually Calcutta with fondness, but those were tumultuous years, and he was surrounded by a welter of events and circumstances that swirled around him like tidal waves. He was born in a particularly fraught moment in his nation's history, and his young mind came to maturity in years of severe upheavals and transformation.

He could not see it at the time but calm reflection quite often rationalises what it does not romanticise when it looks back on a long, important life. It imposes patterns on events and certain moments seem to positively glow with retrospective significance. All the complex currents of life that seem so random and chaotic resemble a clear narrative with a predetermined end.

Soumitra Chatterjee was born on a cold winter night on 19 January 1935 in Calcutta. It was new moon in the city but the pervasive gloom was happily dispelled for Mohitkumar and Ashalata Chatterjee at the birth of their second child. Ashalata, an educated woman whose love for music and literature was to play a pivotal role in his youth, named him after 'Soumitri Keshori' from Michael Madhusudan Dutt's epic poem, *Meghnadbadh Kabya*.

He was born at a time of great turmoil. The country was on the cusp of independent nationhood, caught up in the throes of historical process and change. In the West, the great balance of power that had determined the history of the world for centuries stood on the brink. Soumitra's early years were witness to events of tremendous national and international significance.

When the Western world finally went to war again in 1939, it dragged its colonies into it with practised callousness. In India, the struggle for independence was launching its final triumphant offensive against the crumbling edifice of colonial rule. The myriad cross currents of history, clashing and converging, led inevitably to 1947. This historic moment was witnessed by twelve-year-old Soumitra, and he remembers the tremendous euphoria that surrounded that moment in August when they could call themselves free. It is not surprising that Soumitra could never see himself as a self-sufficient aesthete separate from the socio-political currents of the society he lived in. He never jettisoned this sense of social responsibility later, even when it would have been more convenient to do so.

The family moved to Krishnanagar soon after he was born. He spent a fair part of his formative years there. His grandfather, Lalitkumar Chatterjee, had moved to Krishnanagar from Kaya, a village in Kusthia district near Selaidaha, famous for the estate of Maharshi Debendranath Tagore (now in Bangladesh), where they used to live in their ancestral home, *Basanta Villa*. Lalitkumar built a new house after he moved to Krishnanagar and named it *Sudha Niloy*. This is where he lived until his father's work took him to other parts of Bengal.

Among the many things Soumitra recalls from this time, the most enduring memories are of Bagha Jatin, the celebrated freedom fighter who also happened to be his father's nephew. Jatindranath Mukherjee's short career as an incendiary revolutionary had quickly turned him into a legendary figure, an exemplar of bravery and strength far beyond the normal or even the possible. The young Soumitra sat wide-eyed, listening to stories of how he had fought and killed a tiger in the jungles of Koya. The story goes that he had been on the lookout for a leopard that had been causing damage to property and livestock in the village when he came upon a fierce Royal Bengal tiger. He fought the vicious animal barehanded and was grievously scratched all over, until he plunged a *kukri* in its neck and killed it. He had been badly mauled and it was touch and go for a while as the poison coursed through his body. He was eventually saved by the ministrations of the famous surgeon Lt Col. Suresh Sarbadhikari. The surgeon was so impressed by this feat that he wrote an article about him in the English press, ensuring recognition by the Bengal government and the sobriquet 'Bagha'. It is a story that reminded one of ancient folk tales. This episode soon blended with his other acts as a freedom fighter to create a heroic, semi-mythical figure in the imagination of the young boy.

His grandfather was a radical as well, and had served time as one of the accused in the Howrah-Gang case orchestrated by Bagha Jatin. This charismatic leader of a loosely organised band of revolutionaries eventually met his end in characteristic fashion – like an outlaw of the American frontier. In 1915, he was smoked out of hiding when the British found out his whereabouts through a complicated series of spy relays. He and his companions hid in the forest of Mayurbhanj for two days, eluding capture by a whisker. The British in hot pursuit were joined by local villagers, who had been promised a reward for the capture of a feared bandit. Bagha Jatin, despairing of escape, decided to make his last stand in a makeshift trench on a low hill in Balasore. As the well-armed police and army surrounded him, his companions urged him to get away while they protected his rear. He refused and, armed with nothing more than mauser pistols, the five of them kept the pursuing force at bay for a good seventy-five minutes. The end was nonetheless a foregone conclusion. Bagha Jatin succumbed to his wounds the next day.

Soumitra heard these stories again and again not just as a legacy of his family but also because it inspired patriotic fervor. The same spirit that the dejected Viceroy Minto in the wake of the assassinations of several important officials perpetrated by Bagha Jatin in 1910 had called one of 'anarchy and lawlessness' was exhilarating and exciting beyond measure for an adolescent boy.

He remembers a man who worked as his grandfather's copying clerk at Krishnanagar court – Nibarun Mazumder or, as they used to call him, Keru dadu. A spruce man with a sprightly gait, he was an underground radical who held him and his friends in thrall with tales of his exploits. There were hardly any stories in his young life devoid of deeper social or political purpose.

In his later years Soumitra has spoken at length about the importance of education in the formative years of an actor, and indeed of any artist. It is not necessarily the kind of education that you get in classrooms though. He always talks about being a good observer of reality, actively absorbing the vivid currents of life that surrounds him. Acting is not much different from other arts when it comes to convincing people of the truth of representation. A writer should not write about things he knows nothing about, and an actor would be entirely unconvincing unless he has observed mankind in some detail.

Soumitra speaks admiringly of Tulsi Chakraborty, a maverick genius who despite having no formal training, was an exceptionally gifted performer. He remembers asking him how he is so convincing in his roles. Tulsi apparently said that he does no more than effectively mimic people whom he has seen in similar situations in real life. Soumitra thinks that this is deceptively simple, mostly because it underplays innate fully developed instincts. He maintains that it is important for an artist to be like a watchful and empathetic student, to first see life in the round and then glean what can later be used for higher artistic ends from those experiences.

When he was eight years old, a disastrous famine hit Bengal in 1943, leaving millions dead in its wake. It was an artificial calamity, created in part due to the stringent and ruthless policies of Churchill's war cabinet caught in a desperate tussle for survival in Europe. While the British maintained that there was no famine, the starving and wretched poor haunted the roads of Krishnanagar like skeletal wraiths.

He remembers the streets littered with corpses, and the agonising voices crying for food all around him. He was deeply moved and would try to give them whatever food he could get from the kitchen. There was strict rationing during the war years, and he remembers standing in queue with his elder brother holding slips waiting for their turn. It was a hard schooling in want, starvation and death which he never forgot. Decades later, when Ray made the film *Ashani Sanket* in 1973, he portrayed a desperately poor Brahmin with striking authenticity, turning a painful memory into a plangent record of a terrible time in the nation's history.

Yet for all this, his childhood was one of carefree joys and unbridled mischief. Soumitra, or Pulu as he was called, was boisterous, quick to take offence and even quicker to blows at the slightest provocation. He had modelled himself on people not known for backing down, and so young Pulu the conqueror took on all comers with all the self-conscious bravery of the heroes of his favourite stories. As reports of his brawling multiplied, his distressed parents tried their best to rein in his boisterous rowdiness with stern discipline. It never quite worked though. Pulu, generally high-spirited, and dishevelled with crumpled half-tucked shirt and raggedy trousers disdained both shoes and attempts to curb him in equal measure. His grandfather would greatly disapprove of his slovenliness. He did not like him gadding about town in his bare feet. It was too unbecoming, and he worried that his feet would get bent out of shape. But Pulu was a stubborn little scamp who would do just what he wanted.

He was a child of the country, out in the sun and rain, bobbing in the streams like a young tadpole, and scrambling up the trees like a squirrel. He would sail across the lazy, turbid Jalangi in a boat to reach half-drowned fields swaying lazily in the harvest breeze. There he and his friends would glut themselves with the sweet green peas and run the gamut of the fields through the narrow pathways that blinked in and out of the unending seas of green on all sides. Sometimes, he would climb down the columns of the railway bridge, and lie in wait under tracks until a train would pass by. There under the deafening clatter of a locomotive rushing over the bridge at full tilt, the sun flickering rapidly over his face, Pulu felt an exhilaration that he remembers as if it were yesterday. And when it was summer, he would be found in mango orchards, hanging precariously from branches, looting the trees with the complete abandon of childhood.

His parents found it difficult to control him but they found a way. The only way to keep him quiet was to hand him a book. His parents were voracious readers and imposed no restriction on their son when it came to reading. Consequently, Pulu grew up with an indiscriminate but insatiable appetite for books.

His father would buy bestsellers as soon as they would hit the stand, and Pulu could not wait to run his fingers through the pages and smell the unmistakable new book smell. He sat alone in corners, absorbed for hours in well-thumbed tomes with yellowing dog-eared pages, sometimes forgetting the games of hide and seek that had enticed him to those corners in the first place.

Through the years, he managed to read a vast range of books in Bengali and English, the classics jostling with bestsellers, stories for children and other books on a wide array of subjects. His parents by not regulating what he read had inculcated in him a love for reading itself, a curiosity that grew more and more unquenchable as he continued to read extensively.

Later he would recall being especially enamoured of the houses of relatives that had libraries. Sir Ashutosh Mukherjee's (his paternal aunt's house) large, very well-stocked library in Calcutta was a favourite, and he also remembers Sourindromohan Mukhopadhyay (his mother's uncle) with great fondness because he would quite often gift him books to encourage his love for reading.

Pulu slowly developed a taste for realism in literature, which considering his general experience, was not exactly surprising. He also remained a devoted student of the two national epics, *Ramayana* and *Mahabharata*, all his life. He was introduced to them through Upendrakishore Ray Chowdhury's version for children. Later he studied the serious translations of Rajsekhar Basu and Kaliprasanna Sinha. He has gone back to these epics several times in his life, zealously sifting them for deeper and profounder insights. He looks upon them as the repositories of the shared wisdom of his country's culture, acquired over long generations of experience and strife. There is compensation and comfort to be found if one searches hard enough. They have not disappointed him yet. 'A lifetime is not nearly enough to fully appreciate what these epics have to say,' he adds.

The greatest influence on his life, by his own admission, has been that of Rabindranath Tagore. His earliest memories of him are of the day the poet passed away. He was eight and had stayed back home from school due to a lingering fever. Sambit, his elder brother, came back early. He told the family that they had closed the school down in mourning because Tagore had passed away. He recalls that a pall of immeasurable gloom descended on the house. It was as if his brother had brought news of a death in the family. He vividly remembers a distraught Ashalata holding on to the railings as she slowly slipped down to the floor. He had known then that someone very important had died, and he never lost that awed reverence which he had witnessed around him that fateful day.

When he was very small, Tagore songs that were used in films and sung by Pankaj Mullick or K.L. Saigal or Kanan Devi were played around town. He did not understand the words but would still be charmed by the melody of the steady rhythmic lines. He remembers how it would fill him with a strange melancholy that he could not really understand. Tagore had made early inroads into his fledgling heart and this bond forged in innocence remained a steadfast one all through his life.

As he grew in comprehension, he learnt to find consolation in Rabindrasangeet. He would sing them to himself whenever he was distressed, a habit he never abandoned. When he was in college, his maternal uncle was diagnosed with cancer. He used to sit by his bedside and sing Tagore songs in a low, melodious voice. He was singing *'Dukkho jodi na pabe to dukkho tomar ghuchbe kobe'* ('If you do not taste sorrow how will sorrow ever end') one day, when he saw tears in his uncle's eyes. He paused, wondering if the song had caused him anguish. His uncle bade him continue and he sang *'Sesh nahi je sesh katha ke bolbe'* ('As nothing is final, so none can speak the last word'). He later said that at that moment when he closed his eyes while singing, he had a vision of the poet himself awaiting his uncle's imminent death by his bedside. Tagore has always been for him a source of the greatest solace and consolation in the darkest of times.

Pulu's great love for literature would probably have made him a diligent scholar if not for a strong performative streak in him. Later in his life, he is very clear about this distinction. It is not always possible for a scholar to be an artist, he says. It is difficult to disagree. His youth was spent in absorbing books and experiences of all kinds. It would eventually all come out in creative outpouring one way or another. It is the way he was built really, mostly because literature was never too far from performance in his childhood.

His mother was no singer, but she would recite with a sweet, carefully cadenced rhythm. He would fall asleep to her recitations from *Shishu*, a collection of poems and lullabies for children. It would thrill him to think that *'Brishti pore tapur tupur / Nodey elo ban…'* ('Pitter, patter goes the rain / The river is in spate…') which his mother would recite once put a very young

Rabindranath to sleep as well. This is where his love for poetry began. In a few years, barely into his teens, he would be writing poetry himself.

Mohitkumar worked in Calcutta and visited his family during the weekend. Pulu looked forward eagerly to the end of the week. They would work together on relief maps using clay and paint and, even more importantly, he would sit them down and recite *Debotar Grash*, Tagore's poetic indictment of superstition and priesthood. *Debotar Grash* starts with a pilgrimage undertaken by a representative group of people (symbolic of Bengali society in particular) that in a moment of crisis degenerates into anarchy leading to the sacrifice of an innocent young man in a bid to appease an angry god. Mohitkumar knew how to exploit the dramatic potential of this deeply moving story. He would expertly modulate the tenor of his deep baritone voice, slowly intensifying the dread and tension until the final heart-wrenching moment that leaves the world in chaotic darkness. Pulu would sit enraptured, moved to tears.

He understood what the right performance can do to transform words on a page to a living reflection of human nature in all its complexity. He lay awake several nights trying to wrap his head around the world of the poem that was familiar and yet so very unfamiliar – its beliefs, its capacity for compassion and hatred, and its biases and its superstitions. Later he knew that it had been part of an evolving process in which he continuously strove to understand the wellsprings of motivation that determined so much of the behaviour of his countrymen.

Irrespective of what eventually transpired, Pulu's first foray into the world of acting was only really a matter of time. It suits a biographer's sense of dramatic necessity to identify a particular moment when his subject takes a decision that settles the course of his life. And while he would do exactly that once he met Sisir Bhaduri, it did not come out of nowhere. In young Pulu's case, it was not even a decision he had to take. Krishnanagar had a long, rich cultural history, which included the prominent early modern 19th-century Bengali playwright, Dwijendralal Ray. His deeply influential legacy led to the founding of several theatrical groups in his hometown that were still largely operational when Pulu was growing up. Besides, Mohitkumar was passionate about theatre and his grandfather was the president of a local theatrical group.

He began at home, acting in skits, and then quickly started performing in plays put up at schools and around the locality. He had a natural talent for it, and he graduated to acting in Tagore's one-act plays like *Dakghar* (Post Office) and *Mukut* (The Crown). Soon he was a local favourite, a veritable child star of the petite stages of Krishnanagar. He got a number of medals out of it too, which further stoked the fires of this nascent passion. He loved the adulation of the audience. He cherishes those medals he got as a child more than the numerous awards that have come his way in later years. 'They are not about my acting really,' he maintains. The medals came directly from the appreciation of the audience. It is a belief strong enough in him to practically be a principle that his greatest reward and the primary cause of his longevity has been the unwavering loyalty of the paying audience. He states quite unequivocally that he would not have lasted as long as he has if the audience had turned its back on him. The long intervening years that separate his amateur beginnings at Krishnanagar and his present indisputable stature as a performer are smoothly bridged by this keen understanding of what constitutes an artist's real rewards.

He remembers how an episode in those years left a lasting impact on him. He was in the fifth standard at school when he was selected to act in an English play, *The Sleeping Princes,* directed by Miss McArthur, the American principal of CMS St John's School, Krishnanagar. A British gentleman she was hosting was acting as consultant. He spoke at length about how a performance can be made authentic by a close observation of people in similar situations in real life. 'If you want to play a man desperately hungry,' he said, 'I suggest that the next time you see a hungry man, you observe everything about him rather closely.' Even though many decades have passed since then, Soumitra still marks this as the moment he began his long education as an actor.

As he grew older, he began to take on more challenging roles. In 1951, he played Sir John Clavering in *Maharaja Nandakumar* to great acclaim among his peers. For his performance as Karna in *Naranarayan* Kailashnath Katju, the Governor of West Bengal, rewarded him with yet another medal.

Long before he left his idyllic childhood in Krishnanagar behind and followed his father to Calcutta, Soumitra had developed a passionate interest in acting. Krishnanagar had history and its fair share of culture, and while it did well for itself, it had all the parochial limitations of a small town anywhere in the world. When he came to the big city, the possibilities and opportunities of the great metropolis changed his life. He was exposed to a wide array of influences that shaped him in ways that would decide the kind of man he eventually became. In time, a chance encounter with Sisir Bhaduri, the greatest thespian of his generation, would finally turn his amateur interest in acting into a true vocation.

His years at Krishnanagar had prepared him in ways that he could never have understood at the time. It is really hindsight that is fond of looking at the past as a kind of narrative with a neat little structure. Like a well-written script, it has its plot points and every event becomes an easily recognisable step that points at the end. It would be easy to look upon his time with Sisir Bhaduri as that first important plot point that settled the course of his life. Things are never probably that explicit and obvious when they happen though. The cross currents of his childhood had primed him well for his future life even before he met the great man. The latter was really more a catalyst than anything else. Soumitra does not disagree. In fact, when he looks back now, he is quite convinced that if his childhood had been any different, he would never have been an actor.

Soumitra remained deeply rooted in his cultural milieu all his life. He was a Bengali who understood Bengal well because all of its history, values, culture and art had gone into the making of him. He knew how the bearing of a man, the stifled smile or the suppressed tear, the fitful play of myriad emotions in a passing glance, can do much to reveal the truth of a person's reality. This is what he spent the rest of his life trying to portray on celluloid. Acting was not simply about being a convincing impersonator. It was about capturing something hidden deep underneath the bustle and fever of everyday life – truths of humanity, high and low, caught in the struggle of life itself. His performances, like a poem or a painting, are meant to be a medium through which these truths are expressed.

YOUTH AND SISIR KUMAR BHADURI

In Calcutta, Soumitra's mind opened up to horizons wide and teeming with opportunity and excitement. He had lived in Howrah for a while and had witnessed the horrors of Partition. His memories of the time are of unalloyed fear, a veritable nightmare come true for an eleven-year-old boy. It was a difficult era, and there were many of his generation then who had to grow up before their time. When he eventually moved to Calcutta in 1951, the city was not entirely new to him. He would travel there from time to time from Howrah, and while he was not overwhelmed by it, he was certainly very excited at the prospect of living there. Calcutta was the great metropolis of the east, the erstwhile second city (after London) of the British empire. There was history lurking in every corner, and then there was that heady feeling of being in the big city, a gateway to the rest of the world. He liked the bustle of life there, its immense size, the baffling yet intriguing possibilities of experience at every turning, its snaking, complicated alleys and its wide, expansive thoroughfares. It was bright, big, a little frightening and alluring at the same time, and it filled his young mind with eager anticipation.

The year he moved to Calcutta, he joined City College on Amherst Street to pursue an honours degree in Bengali literature. He would later follow this up with an MA from Calcutta University. There was a whole city to explore, and he and his new friends walked the length and breadth of it, absorbing every bit of it in those years.

One of his professors in college was the famous writer Narayan Gangopadhyay, whose greatest and enduring fame lies in that supreme comic creation, Tenida. Prof. Gangopadhyay had a way with words and Soumitra remembers how any text he touched would come alive. He had a dramatic flair too. He once recounted this story about Bankim Chandra Chattopadhyay and a young Rabindranth Tagore. They had called Bankim babu to felicitate him, and Tagore was there on the podium. The veteran doyen of Bengali literature took the garland off his neck and proceeded to felicitate an abashed Tagore. He paused at the end of the story and then said, 'The crescent moon of the waning night greeted the rising sun of the new dawn...' Soumitra was entirely smitten with his panache, and he would sit in the class thinking that his lectures had all the grace and appeal of literature in their own right.

He learnt from his friends too. He says that it is during this time that he was lucky enough to have friends who gave him much needed direction. He was always an indiscriminate reader. He credits Gourmohan Mukhopadhyay, one of his seniors at college and later a reputed professor of Bengali himself, with instilling in him a certain amount of discipline when it came to reading. Soumitra was spurred on to read as much as he could. College Street was not too far from his college, and he spent a number of afternoons browsing around the footpaths strewn and quite often overflowing with books on all conceivable subjects. And then it was on to the famous Coffee House right around the corner. Coffee House was where everyone with the slightest intellectual pretensions would end up in those glory days of the argumentative Bengali. You could spend hours having heated discussions about any topic under the sun, and no one would shoo you away. The waiters in uniforms and slightly comical turbans would walk by languidly when you did not need them, and refuse to look at you when you tried to frantically get their attention. But it did not matter. You could order a small cup of the strangest, darkest black coffee that they would call an infusion, and hold forth on the topic du jour until it was time to close down. For Soumitra these were happy, carefree days, and his natural exuberance and keen curiosity made him an opinionated young man not very different from many like him hanging out at Coffee House. He had all the confidence of youth, bubbling over with questions, judgments and views about everything he thought were the important questions of life. It did not matter what the argument was, he was not about to back down just as he had never backed down from a fight in the dusty lanes of Krishnanagar.

You can see him at one of the tables, lanky, sharp-featured, with a ready smile and loud ideas, passionately declaiming as if his life depended on it. These discussions would inevitably take a political turn, which in the first decade of a hard-won independence was not very surprising. He was barely seven years old when the Quit India movement spread across the country. Demonstrations, protest marches and mob violence radiated out from Calcutta and Dacca to the suburbs and right to his doorstep. Between that and the traumatic memories of the Partition, the destiny of this new nation had a deep, personal relevance for him and his friends.

He did not think that he could afford to be detached or cynical. Soumitra belonged to the first adult generation of a free nation, and he had a fairly heightened sense of social responsibility. He remembers being passionately invested in the dream of freedom, of independence from a distant land that had imprisoned his grandfather and killed Bagha Jatin, the greatest hero of his childhood days. He celebrated when Jawaharlal Nehru spoke of India's tryst with destiny and raised for the first time the tricolour over the Lahori Gate in Delhi's Red Fort on 15 August 1947. Disillusionment was to follow soon.

They spent long weeks and months talking about independence and whether it was worth it. Were they free from poverty and hunger? What had this independence done for the average poor man really? The toiling masses remained desperately poor. Their lives continued to be a frantic struggle for survival. It distressed him to see how very little had changed from the days those starving skeletal specters from his childhood during the great famine of 1943 died in their thousands. It was a false independence, he concluded, in which the lives of the poor and the dispossessed remained unchanged.

He started reading Marx and Engels fervently, finding in their dialectical vision of history, an answer to the problems that he now understood as endemic in society. He has remained a dedicated Marxist, even though his experience has taught him that mankind has to evolve a lot more for a classless society to be a reality. He has turned to it from time to time for solace as much as he has depended on Tagore to get him through moments of despondency. It also convinced him that form and content in art must necessarily emerge from the historical, economic and social realities of a civilisation.

A couple of months before his final university examination, he took up a job at All India Radio (AIR) as a staff artist. It was not meant to be serious, and eventually he rejected several offers including one from AIR, New Delhi. He was initially reluctant to take part in radio plays because he did not think that as a form it had any real artistic scope. He did nevertheless learn a few things about using the microphone. He understood the importance of pitch and even distance from mike to achieve the desired effect. He learnt from Nilima Sanyal and Jayanta Chowdhury, two very popular radio artists, the quality of volume and timbre required to create a soothing yet clear tone. He was deeply impressed by their lack of pretension and clarity of diction. He studied how they delivered deeply nuanced performances through voice alone.

It did inspire him to do a couple of radio plays eventually. There are many who remember his performances in *Nirupam Yatra* and *Threepenny Novel*. The former was based on a storyline by Jibanananda Das, and dramatised by Soumyadeb Basu, and the latter was an adaptation of Bertolt Brecht's musical by Rama Prasad Banik. Nevertheless, his first love was still theatre and it was not long before he quit radio.

His restless energies scampered off in all directions, and just as books had once reined him in, his love for acting was soon to decide the eventual course of his life. Gourmohan, who had done much to refine his uncritical reading, decided one day to take him to a play. He thought that it was a crying shame that a man who calls himself intelligent and culturally aware has never seen Sisir Bhaduri perform on stage. It was meant to round off his education. It did more than that. It led to a lot of soul-searching and a momentous decision.

The play they went to see was Kshirode Prasad Vidyavinode's *Alamgir*, which happened to be the production with which Sisir Kumar Bhaduri had started his career. It is difficult now to get a proper critical estimation of his legendary skill. The popular press at the time had this peculiar habit of describing everything in the most hyperbolic and ludicrous terms possible.

They would compare him to all the famous actors in the world to their disadvantage at considerable length. Then they would happily conclude that Bengali theatre was miles ahead of the contemporary British or American theatre. Each performance would be greeted by fawning critics with hysterical praise. Speaking of his performance in *Sita* one of them wrote, 'Not Ram, but it was Sisir Kumar they had wanted to see, the human being garbed in the guise of God, whom they were eager to hail and if possible to touch his feet.' The same was true for his performance as the troubled Mughal emperor Aurangzeb in *Alamgir*. The better ones among them would mostly write of the effect of his performance on them. It was hypnotic and it would leave the audience awed or stunned.

Soumitra recalls being completely unprepared for what he was about to see and what it would do to him. It was thoroughly overwhelming. As Sisir Bhaduri slowly built this complex character from scratch with his studied skill, uncovering layer after layer, the audience was fully tricked into believing that it was not an actor but the character itself that had come to life. His voice was mesmerising, Soumitra recalls, and his Aurangzeb was a complete triumph. He vividly remembers Aurangzeb desperately trapped in a fortified hill, parched to the bone, barely able to speak, and staring at imminent death. Sisir Kumar's rousing portrayal stirred him so profoundly that he knew with conviction that this was art of the highest order.

He came back home from the theatre barely able to fully articulate the elation and excitement that he felt. All other thought had been banished from his mind, and he spent sleepless nights obsessing over Sisir Kumar's performance, the sheer mastery of which slowly turned into a governing ambition. He later claimed that that one night completely changed the way he looked at life. Or perhaps it had reoriented it so that it had a purpose.

When the fever of it had passed and given way to calm reflection, he had no doubt about what he wanted to do for the rest of his life. He made up his mind that he would be a professional actor.

The clarity of the moment, which sounds so much like an incident in a well-written narrative, might seem a little glib. It is possible that his subsequent relationship with Sisir Bhaduri, whom he adores to this day, along with everything he learnt from him has coloured his memories of the time he saw him for the first time. There is however no doubting the sincerity of his decision. From that point onwards, there was no looking back for Soumitra Chatterjee, the actor.

The day Soumitra met Sisir Bhaduri for the first time was a sad one for the thespian. Srirangam, which he had established in 1942, and tended with meticulous care, was shutting down that night after a final performance of Girish Chandra Ghosh's *Prafulla*. Soumitra was lucky because Shefalika Putul (she would play Aparna's mother in *Apur Sansar*), his friend's mother, and a mainstay of the group, took him backstage before the performance.

Later that evening, right before the curtains would come down for the last time, surrounded by his heartbroken troupe members waiting in the wings and backstage, Sisir Bhaduri as Jogesh uttered the last dialogue of the play – '*Amar sajano bagan shukiye gelo*' (The garden I tended for years has now withered away).

He was an old man when a friendship developed between him and Soumitra. He was at the twilight of an immensely popular and influential career. Sisir Bhaduri had come to Bengali theatre at a critical moment in its history. Ever since the establishment of the first public stage in Calcutta in 1872, the city had been the nerve centre of Bengali drama. In the last decade of colonial rule, however, it had degenerated to a point that the educated class had effectively stopped patronising the theatres in the city. The native *jatra* that preceded the westernised theatre had strong roots. *Jatra* continued to be the most popular form of dramatic entertainment in the rural reaches of Bengal. In the city, the theatre was overrun by plays that were facile. They unashamedly pandered to the prevailing appetite for rampant sensationalism and overwrought patriotism. The theatre was marked by vulgarity, emotional excesses and uncontrolled sentimentality. It was dismissed as entertainment for the rabble, without any real seriousness. Sisir Kumar changed all that.

Sisir Kumar studied in Presidency College, Calcutta (now Presidency University), where he earned an MA in English literature, and spent some years as a professor of English at the Metropolitan College (now Vidyasagar College). He was greatly influenced by the dramatic realism of Henrik Ibsen and George Bernard Shaw. He was an exceptionally gifted actor, who all through his career drew large crowds on the strength of his name on the bill alone. He was the biggest star of his time.

Yet the bulk of his reputation in retrospect lies in his contribution to theatre as a whole. Sisir Bhaduri was not the first great actor of the Bengali stage, but he was the first to reform every aspect of the theatre. He was keen on importing the social realism that he had seen in the 'little theatres' of Europe. He abandoned the elaborate Victorian stage designs with wings on both sides, and footlights as the only sources of lighting. He commissioned more realistic box sets and put up lights for zonal illumination. He instructed his actors to bring in a degree of psychological naturalism in their performances, steadily reducing verbal flourishes and rhetorical extravagance. He took an active interest in every aspect of the theatrical experience, looking into music, dancing, backdrops, costumes with meticulous attention to the slightest detail.

In October 1956, Soumitra and a couple of friends, extremely excited at the prospect of meeting Sisir Bhaduri, walked a fairly long distance from Shyambazar to his home in north Calcutta. It was his birthday, but no one else apart from them had come that day. Their host was gracious, and even though almost half a century separated him from Soumitra, he allowed the eager, young man to return again and again.

Sisir Bhaduri was the first real mentor in Soumitra's life. He had long discussions with Sisir Bhaduri about theatre, and especially about acting. He started observing his performances as a serious student of the craft. He had already decided that he would be an actor, and this was his first real education. He would later say that Sisir Bhaduri's wide exposure to world theatre allowed him to see the dominant trend towards greater realism in dramatic representation. This in no small measure decided his own attitude towards acting. He would spend the rest of his career trying to inhabit the psychological reality of the person he's portraying.

Sisir Bhaduri had the deepest respect for his predecessors. He believed that Girish Chandra Ghosh was the greatest actor in Bengali theatre, and he admired people like Durgadas Bandyopadhyay, Tinkari Chakrabarty, Nirmalendu Lahiri and Ahindra Chowdhury among others. In spite of his love for contemporary European theatre he never wavered in his loyalty to his native tradition. He knew that it had lost its way and he took it upon himself to infuse seriousness of purpose and modern relevance into it.

He controlled theatricality of expression on stage by placing greater emphasis on modulation of voice and delivery. He would say that when the manner overwhelms the words, then the latter lose their meaning. Soumitra recalls how he would talk about tonal manner being a shadow of what is being expressed. He remembers seeing this in action when he saw his mentor play Jibanananda in *Soroshi*, where he used subtle variations in delivery to express very different things. When he spoke through the agony of cirrhosis with a clenched face, it was slow and straight, almost staccato in its bareness. Yet when he spoke to his wife, Alaka, there would be a hint of a lilt, a softening of tone. He would incorporate these shifts so delicately that they would intensify the meaning without disrupting the illusion of naturalism.

Sisir Bhaduri severely discouraged imitation, no matter how tempting it might be. He would constantly help his actors to find out what would suit the character best, and his little bits of advice and notes would prove invaluable to the company. He would ask Soumitra to build a character from scratch, visualise him in the main and in general. Place him in the context of the story. Every dialogue he says, has a logic behind it.

'Follow the logic and you can never go wrong,' was his advice.

Soumitra took all this to heart, always closely reading scripts to identify the context in which to place his characters, constantly searching for their inner reality and using all his technical acumen to convincingly express it. He would follow this advice diligently while preparing to play Apu in his first film. He has no qualms about saying that everything that he knows about acting comes from his association with his first mentor.

A year after Srirangam closed down, Sisir Bhaduri decided to stage *Prafulla* at the Banga Sanskriti Sammelan in 1957. Soumitra landed up at his house in B.T. Road as soon as he heard the news. He had met him several times by then, but he still found him quite intimidating. He fought his nervousness down and asked him about *Prafulla*.

'Do you want a role in it?'

There was no way Soumitra would ask for it outright.

'Only if you think I'm right for it.'

'I think you are right for Suresh. Get a copy of the play and meet me for rehearsals.'

It was a big day for him and if he had wanted to jump for joy, he did a good job of hiding it.

Rehearsals were happening at a small dimly lit room of a local club in Shyambazar. His company had assembled there and, with barely suppressed excitement, Soumitra threw himself into the process with all the eagerness at his disposal. He remembers reading lines earmarked for Suresh, trying to keep his anxiety at bay. At one point he was supposed to shout at someone but no matter how hard he tried, he could not generate a fuller volume. Sisir Bhaduri asked him to not throttle his voice.

'Use the full range of your vocal chord!'

He thought he had too thin a voice for it. Sisir Bhaduri had looked at him for a while before saying, 'You have a very powerful voice. Unfortunately you don't know it yet.'

He was proved right less than a year later when Soumitra did a voice test for Satyajit Ray. He had chosen *Banshi* by Rabindranath Tagore, a poem that strung together scenes from the life of an ordinary man. It was recorded at Technician's Studio and, later Ray heard it with Niren Lahiri, another film director he had called in for a second opinion. They were both very impressed with the quality of Soumitra's audition.

When it was time to play Suresh on stage, Soumitra was a nervous wreck. He was scared of making mistakes and disappointing his mentor. It was also quickly evident that it was one thing to rehearse with Sisir Bhaduri and quite another to act with him on stage. When Suresh asks his elder brother, Jogesh (played by Sisir Kumar), to stop drinking, he turns back and shouts at him in rage. Soumitra recoiled on stage, shaken straight out of character, by the sheer authenticity and force of his fury. It seemed to him that he had shouted at him and not his character. He was so very out of sorts that it was all he could do to not rush out of the theatre. At the end of the scene, Nivanani Devi, who played Umasashi, Jogesh's mother, cornered him and told him, 'It seemed that you couldn't wait to get away from the stage.' Soumitra nodded mortified, and she told him, 'We are students of Boro Babu (which is how his company referred to Sisir Kumar). We can't afford to make such mistakes.' Soumitra knew that it was a lapse of discipline and understood the invisible strain of simply being in character for the duration of a play.

Theatre became his principal obsession, dominating his every thought and the primary topic of discussion at Coffee House. At the time, students in colleges and universities all over the city were involved in theatre. Soumitra even put together a group of his own, and proceeded to begin what he thought would be his career on stage in earnest.

During one of his discussions with Sisir Kumar, the latter talked to him at length about the German playwright Bertolt Brecht, whom he considered the Shakespeare of the modern era. He even gave Soumitra a copy of Brecht's *The Exception and the Rule* and asked him to adapt it in Bengali. He gave it a shot and Sisir Kumar named it *Bidhi-o-Byatikrom*. It was not a great success, he recalls, because he had been too faithful to the original while his mentor had wanted something different. It did start something else though. Throughout his life, Soumitra would adapt a number of plays from all over the world in Bengali. If at this point, he was thinking of films, it was definitely a secondary concern.

Soumitra does not make any bones about his general disapproval of cinema during this extremely idealistic phase of his life. It was not always like that though. In Krishnanagar, he would save money from what he got for lunch at school and get the one-paisa ticket for the front rows. He was pretty much a fixture there, devouring whatever was released in his town in English, Hindi or

Bengali. He distinctly remembers being deeply affected by *The Yearling* which came out in 1946, a Gregory Peck and Jane Wyman tearjerker about a family trying to pick up the pieces of their life in a farm after the devastation of the Civil War. The unabashedly sentimental yarn took such a hold of his imagination that he could not sleep for a couple of nights.

When he grew up and moved to Calcutta, the wider exposure to culture he got diminished the importance of cinema. Cinema was light entertainment for the masses. It was beneath the serious attention of a dedicated intellectual. It does not really hold up, he decided, when you compare it to theatre. Sisir Kumar too was famously contemptuous of it and, as his ardent disciple, it was only natural that he too would have the same attitude towards cinema. He took his cue from his mentor who, with the exception of the films of Charles Chaplin, did not consider the medium a proper art form. Soumitra later understood that Sisir Kumar was perhaps a little too rigid in his sweeping denunciation of cinema.

Nevertheless, he found it very difficult to treat the melodramatic commercial fare churned out by the contemporary Bengali film industry with any seriousness. It did not aspire to be art and he never condescended to treat it as such. All this was to change with the release of Satyajit Ray's *Pather Panchali* in 1955. Less than five years later, he would play Apu to widespread acclaim in the last film of the trilogy.

Poster of *Apur Sansar* (1959)
Photo courtesy of Ray Society

APUR SANSAR

On 9 August 1958, Soumitra was preparing for his first shot in *Apur Sansar*. Apu, in desperate need of a job, goes to a labelling plant in Beliaghata. In his first scene, Soumitra, umbrella in hand, walks through a narrow, dimly lit passage into an equally dark, claustrophobic room where several people are putting labels on bottles. They work silently and swiftly like automatons, and when one of them looks up at Apu and stares fixedly at him, the protagonist recoils slightly. He is scared that he will end up like one of them and, as he steps back, he gulps in fear.

Soumitra recalls that even though Ray had given him meticulous directions on what to do, he had added that gulp at the last moment. It seemed like something Apu would do at that point. It subtly accentuated the distress in his body language. Ray who never missed the slightest deviation from his instructions, said 'Excellent!' from behind the camera and okayed it. He had nailed it in the first shot.

Soumitra began his acting career at a time of significant changes in the Bengali film industry, and in world cinema in general. While the country got busy with the difficult business of nation building in the first decade after Independence, the Western world was recovering from the ravages of a disastrous war. In 1948, Vittoria de Sica made *Bicycle Thieves*, a heart-wrenching film about a poor man searching for a stolen bicycle, without which his family would face starvation. *Bicycle Thieves* was brutally realistic, wearing its socialist heart on its sleeve. It reflected a seminal shift in cinematic sensibilities in every possible sense, including in acting. It was also to have an extremely important influence on the Indian film industry. As a matter of fact, the revolution that Satyajit Ray and Soumitra Chatterjee brought about in Bengali cinema can barely be understood without placing it in the right context.

In Italy, as the fascist order came tumbling down, the vacuum created was momentarily filled by socialist political organisations. The extremely influential Marxist theorist Antonio Gramsci contented that the ruling capitalist elite retained its dominance by manipulating media and popular culture to push their ideologies. Cesare Zavattini adapted this and came up with neo-realism in cinema, the utilisation of film to point out the inequalities of society. This was cinema with a clear political agenda, but it led to a shift towards realism in representation that greatly influenced contemporary Indian cinema.

In India, cinema that had strong roots in Bombay and Calcutta since the turn of the century depicted mythological stories in an extravagant, histrionic manner. It had come to Calcutta as early as 1897, only a few years after it was introduced in Europe. Calcutta was the greatest city of the British empire after London, an extremely important port, and a melting pot for all kinds of ethnicities and classes of people. While the European part of town would see American and European films in theatres around Chowringhee and the Maidan, a number of theatres catering to the natives began mushrooming further north around Beadon street. The indigenous films made for the latter still owed much to theatre and retained the exaggerated theatrics of the native *jatra*. These films were dismissed as trivial and frivolous by the native intelligentsia, who preferred to watch the English films in the fancy part of town. Consequently, cinema was not serious art, if it was considered art at all. This perception changed gradually due to movements that oddly enough ran along parallel lines in India and Europe.

The strong leftist element in Indian cinema in the 1940s and 50s was due largely to the IPTA (Indian People's Theatre Association), the theatrical wing of the CPI (Communist Party of India). The IPTA had been active ever since the Quit India Movement in 1942. Their political agenda of fostering Hindu–Muslim unity was shattered by the Partition, and they felt betrayed by Jawaharlal

Soumitra shooting for *Apur Sansar*
Photo courtesy of Ray Society

Nehru's gradual socialism, which they were convinced was leading to greater oppression of the marginalised poor. Several members of the IPTA like K.A. Abbas, Prithviraj Kapoor, Balraj Sahni, Ritwik Ghatak and Salil Chowdhury became very important figures in the film industry. It was Abbas's *Dharti Ke Lal* (1946), with the West Bengal famine of 1943 as a backdrop, which first used cinema for social reform. The tone was still melodramatic but the first step had been taken.

In 1956, Bimal Ray made *Do Bigha Zameen*, a relentlessly critical look at the reality of the peasant in post-independent India. Salil Chowdhury wrote the

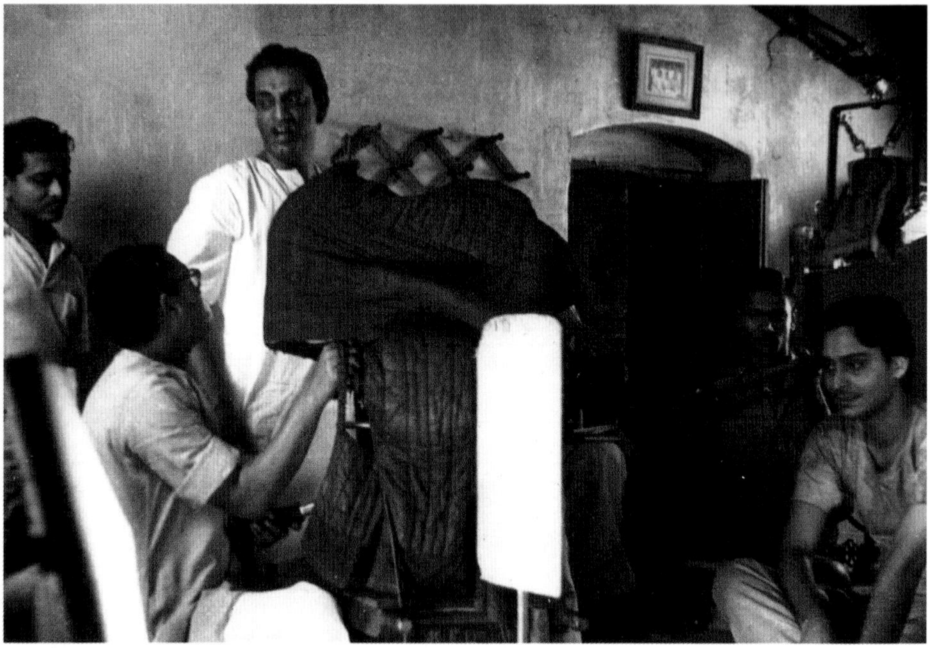

Young, hungry and eager to prove himself – Soumitra on the sets of *Apur Sansar*
Photo courtesy of Ray Society

script, and the lead role was played by Balraj Sahni, both prominent members of the IPTA. Interestingly enough, Soumitra is a self-confessed fan of Balraj Sahni's work, and he says that he learnt a lot from him in his early days.

The story is distinctly informed by De Sica's aesthetics and approach. The protagonist, a farmer named Shambhu Mahato, desperately trying to save his small plot of land in the village from being taken over by people who want to build a mill, comes to the big city. Bimal Ray's urban spaces are frightening and confusing. The city is hostile and apathetic, and crushes Shambhu Mahato and his family like some huge, unfeeling machinery. Bimal Ray did not have complete freedom though. In spite of its convictions and the seriousness of its theme, *Do Bigha Zameen* still had to incorporate some of the populist trappings (like songs) of commercially successful cinema.

This gradual shift towards a socially conscious realism was reflected in acting as well. The Bengali film industry had its share of popular actors, not

Poster of *Apur Sansar*
Photo courtesy of Ray Society

the least among whom were stars like Pramathesh Barua and Kanan Devi. Their approach to acting was theatrical. While it was immensely popular at the time, it might look rather dated and unnatural to the modern viewer. Whatever its merits, it was entirely inappropriate for a realistic narrative. Nonetheless, the evolution of realistic acting was not a natural part of the growing trend of realism in cinema. The emergence of naturalism in acting in the context of world cinema was due to something very different.

In the early twentieth century, a theatre practitioner, Konstantin Stanislavski, came up with a methodology for actors to follow, which came to be known as the 'system'. It was a complicated process that tried to create the illusion of authenticity in performance. The actor will have to mine his own memories, experience and imagination and inhabit the internal and external world of the characters as if they were real people. This was modified further in America by Lee Strasberg and Stella Adler who concentrated on different aspects of the 'system', which was now being called the 'method'. The first important actors to follow the method in America were Montgomery Clift and James Dean. Unfortunately, the former's career was severely hampered by an accident that ruined his face and drove him to alcoholism and an early grave, and the latter's extremely promising start ended with his tragic death at the age of twenty-four in a car crash. Marlon Brando, one of Stella Adler's most promising pupils, emerged as the most significant exponent of the 'method', and eventually left a legacy that continues to this day. Brando's performance on Broadway in 1947 as Stanley

English language poster of *Apur Sansar*
Photo courtesy of Ray Society

The harmonious joy of reunion at the end of *Apur Sansar*
Photo courtesy of Ray Society

Kowalski in Tennessee Williams's *A Streetcar Named Desire* was a searing tour de force of realism. Everything before Brando seemed slightly stiff and artificial.

This transition in Bengali cinema was portrayed effectively in Satyajit Ray's *Nayak*. Ray did not cast Soumitra in the film because he wanted to play off the superstardom of Uttam Kumar in a role that was written for him. Uttam Kumar plays Arindam Mukherjee, an ageing matinee idol caught in a moment of crisis. In one of the many flashbacks in *Nayak*, we see a very young Arindam in his first film acting with Mukunda Lahiri (played by Bireswar Sen), an arrogant older man whose formidable reputation rested on the prevailing theatrical mode of acting. Arindam is understated, and Mukunda rudely interrupts him mid-shot. He is contemptuous of this new fashion in acting, and dismisses it outright. Later Arindam, in an important scene, asserts with all the courage of his convictions that he knew it in his bones that he was right. This was the way of the future.

Soumitra, who would lead the vanguard of this new way, was largely contemplating a career on the stage when *Pather Panchali* released. It was based on a novel of the same name by Bibhutibhushan Bandyopadhyay. During their many sessions at the Coffee House, Soumitra and his friends would talk at length about the novel that had come out in 1928. It was followed by a sequel, *Aparajito* in 1932. These two books would be turned into three films (*Pather Panchali, Aparajito* and *Apur Sansar*) by Ray.

Bibhutibhushan's novel was a great favourite of theirs and their curiosity was piqued when they heard that the film was being helmed by Sukumar Ray's son. Satyajit Ray, who had trained at Visva-Bharati university, started his career as an illustrator for advertising agencies and publishers. He had quickly garnered a bit of a reputation because Soumitra remembers his illustrations for *Aam Antir Bhenpoo*, a number of book covers, and visuals for an ad campaign. Deeply interested in cinema, he saw nearly a hundred films in London, when he got the opportunity to stay there for three months. Among these films was *Bicycle Thieves*. Ray would later say that by the time the film was over, he had decided that he would be a filmmaker.

The neo-realist principles of De Sica's masterpiece were transmuted into an uncompromising and deeply moving adaptation of Bibhutibhushan's novel. Satyajit Ray was immediately hailed as a great filmmaker, someone who had the courage to not compromise the artistic integrity of his work by including populist elements which had found their way even into Bimal Ray's *Do Bigha Zameen*.

Soumitra first saw him when he was being felicitated after the success of *Pather Panchali*, at the Senate Hall. He remembers how Ray had begun his address to the audience by stating that he had not been blind to the demands of commercialism at all. He like any filmmaker wanted his films to be seen by as many people as possible. He believed that there were ways of entertaining an audience without having to resort to mainstream trappings. To Soumitra it seemed that Ray was defining a new method and purpose for Bengali cinema, a method that would give the medium much needed seriousness and legitimacy as an art form.

Above left: Scenes of marital bliss in *Apur Sansar* inspired a whole generation to marry early
Photo courtesy of Ray Society
Above right: Soumitra's expressive eyes capturing the desolation of loss in *Apur Sansar*
Photo courtesy of Ray Society

When *Pather Panchali* released in 1955, it quickly became the only topic of conversation at the Coffee House. No one had ever seen anything quite like it. It was both starkly realistic and intensely lyrical in parts. Soumitra says that they did not talk about anything else for days. They watched and rewatched it several times. Ray's film would eventually transcend local boundaries and emerge as a work of international significance. It was a very important film in the evolution of world cinema. It certainly changed Soumitra's views on cinema and what it was capable of. Not surprisingly, he desperately wanted to work with Ray.

He would get this opportunity far sooner than expected. There was a hiccup at the beginning though. He got to know Nityananda Datta, a member of Ray's unit through a friend. Nityananda (or Netai) who would later become fast friends with Soumitra, told him that Ray was casting *Aparajito*, the sequel to his first film, and that he was looking for a new face for Apu. Netai warned him that Ray might not like him for the part, and that he should be prepared for that.

Learning the ropes at the feet of the Master during the shooting of *Apur Sansar*
Photo courtesy of Ray Society

Soumitra did not care. As far as he was concerned, he was lucky to even get to audition for the great man. They were on a bus, on their way to meet Ray, when Netai gave him the once over and asked him to take his spectacles off. Ray talked to him for a long time on that first day. They talked about films, and he asked Soumitra whether he was serious about acting in films. He had made his decision by then, and so it was not a very difficult question to answer.

'You're much too tall though!'

Ray was looking for someone younger, and the role would eventually go to Smaran Ghoshal. Satyajit Ray had a powerful personality which coupled with his deep baritone voice made an immediate impression on the young Soumitra. At the end of that first meeting, Ray told him to keep in touch.

Aparajito released to high critical acclaim, and was widely considered a worthy sequel of the first film. It sparked endless discussions at Coffee House again, and again the haunting beauty of Ray's work mesmerised Soumitra.

As time went by, when Ray did not call him he got a little dejected and wondered if Ray had forgotten him. He began his stint with AIR in 1957, and was laid up for a few weeks with chicken pox. Luckily for him, it left no marks on his face.

Soon after he had recovered, he was at home one day when Subir Hazra came to tell him that Satyajit Ray wanted to see him. When he reached his Lake Avenue house, he noticed that the director was visibly relieved.

'Thank God, you look fine. Someone had told me that you had pockmarks all over your face!'

He was making the final film of the trilogy, which would cover the last half of Bibhutibhushan's *Aparajito*. Ray was cautious and did not promise him anything.

'I might need you. But I can't give you any guarantees.'

He was careful about not raising hopes. Soumitra thought he had perhaps not decided to cast him yet. Later, he would recall his first meeting that had taken place when Ray was casting *Aparajito*. Ray would size up a person's potential during his first conversation with them. He would minutely study their appearance, their bearing, and especially their fluency in Bengali. The last point was of singular importance to him. An actor's way with words when they spoke Bengali played a vital role in his decision to cast them.

Ray invited him to come visit him at the studio. He was shooting *Jalsaghar* and *Parash Pathar* simultaneously. It was a punishing schedule, and Soumitra was awestruck at how Ray managed two films of such widely different tones, themes and genres at the same time. He wandered around the sets of Bansi Chandragupta, and marvelled at his breathtaking set designs and art direction. Bansi Chandragupta and the wunderkind Subrata Mitra were well-known figures for their work on the first two films of the Apu trilogy. Subrata Mitra was only twenty-one and untrained when he shot *Pather Panchali*. He not only learnt on the job but also pioneered the 'bounce technique' of lighting in his first film. Ray always understood the importance of surrounding himself with the right people.

One day when Soumitra had gone to the set of *Jalsaghar*, Ray asked him if he wanted to meet the veteran actor, the legendary Chhabi Biswas. It turned out to be a memorable encounter in more ways than one. Ray introduced him

Polish film poster of *Apur Sansar*

Photo courtesy of Ray Society

by saying, 'Chhabi da, this is Soumitra Chattopadhyay! He's playing Apu in my next film, *Apur Sansar*!' His dream had come true, and his heart was fit to burst with elation and excitement. He later remembered how everything around him had seemed to slow down. On his way back in the bus, he could not believe that it was not hurtling ahead like a missile.

Soumitra remembers how the character of Apu resonated with the young men of his generation in a profound way. 'Everyone used to come up to me and say that it was like watching their own selves on screen. Even Sunil Gangopadhyay, who used to join us at Coffee House often in those days, once told me that he was Apu.'

Apu lives in poverty in a ramshackle rented room in Calcutta. He is surrounded by urban ugliness on all sides, but he is irrepressibly idealistic. His face lights up with joyous smiles when he talks about poetry. He spurns materialism and lives for a life of the mind and of the spirit. The fresh-faced Soumitra, classically handsome with a genteel, sensitive face was perfect for the part. And he gave his all to it.

Ray had prepared copious notes on the character to help a nervous Soumitra in his first film. He recalls that it was not very difficult to get under the skin of the character because the script itself was so meticulously detailed. After the death of his wife, Apu is distraught to the point of distraction. He wanders around the country, and we see him deep in forests, steadily losing himself in rivers and mountains. Torn apart by loss, he stands on a small hill, and flings the pages of his unfinished novel away. Soumitra remembers Ray's script comparing the pages of the manuscript fluttering away to 'an enormous flock of some strange migratory birds disappearing into the depths of the mountain'! He says that there is not much more help you need as an actor with a script like that.

Nevertheless, Soumitra brought a young, ardent passion to his first break. This was an opportunity to implement what he had learnt from Sisir Bhaduri. He went through the script with a fine-toothed comb, searching between the lines for subtle clues and indicators of character. He tried to immerse himself into the character by keeping a small notebook where he would log what he thought Apu was doing or thinking between the events recorded in the script. Ray did not discourage him.

Soumitra's own youthful idealism and artistic ambitions may have informed the character too, and lent that crucial bit of authenticity that made Apu such a believable figure. His co-star Sharmila Tagore began her career as an actress in *Apur Sansar*. Later she reminisced how much she loved his performance when he was talking to his friend as they walked on the train tracks. He recites poetry and talks about being a writer. In his enthusiasm and wide-eyed eagerness, Soumitra captured the dreams and thoughts of an entire generation. Soumitra looked upon Apu as a young man in post-independent India coming to terms with modernity. He was still very green though.

At one point when Apu's friend Pulu comes to visit him in the Chirimiri coal mines, Apu runs up and down a slope to talk to him. Ray told him that he would have to act out of breath. Soumitra decided that he would really have to be out of breath for it to be convincing. He started running up and down, and in his enthusiasm overdid it. The shot went fine, but for a while the crew was a little worried. He smiles now when he remembers his inexperience. Later, he learnt that there are techniques to effectively induce breathlessness without actually having to exert oneself like that. Ray found the whole thing amusing and, in fact, quite liked his dedication.

Ray handled him carefully. This allowed him to not only create a sympathetic, consistent portrayal but also announce his arrival as a major new talent in the industry. There was a raw intensity to his work in this first film. When Apu realises to his horror that his visitor has brought the news of his wife's death, the camera moves in steadily right into his anguish. The enormity of the grief distorts his features. It soon turns into irrational rage as he lunges at the messenger, and then to shock at the violent act so contrary to his nature. Ray keeps the camera on him, and the audience can feel the force of these powerful emotions coursing through the actor's entire frame. A little later in the film, when he throws away his literary ambitions with his manuscript, it is a moment of absolute renunciation. Apu has decided that he will no longer be a part of the world. The desolation he feels is expressed through glance and gesture, no longer through long declamatory speeches or exaggerated displays of emotion. His reunion with his son marks the return of Apu to life and to a new purpose. Soumitra's portrayal of Apu at once established the new manner of acting and set the bar high for others to reach. He also effectively crafted a persona and an identity for the urban, educated Bengali youth of the middle class to emulate. His abhorrence of the mundane, love for literature and idyllic marriage with Aparna (played by Sharmila Tagore) established him as an idealistic, romantic figure at the beginning of his career.

While he was widely praised in contemporary reviews, he is the first to admit that his performance was largely moulded by Ray. He took the young actor under his wing in a way that he would never do again with anyone else. Soumitra took full advantage of it too. He gleaned as much as he could from his encyclopaedic knowledge through long discussions on cinema and literature. He had an active curiosity and Ray was happy to guide him the best way he could. Soumitra has from a very young age looked up to the mentors he chose in his life. He did not have a strongly individualistic streak inclined to rebellion. He rather understood the importance of being an ardent disciple of the right people. And as far as that goes, he did an exceptionally good job of choosing his mentors. It was perhaps serendipitous that he was the right man at the right time. He brought the same seriousness with which he had approached theatre to acting in films. There was the added excitement of doing something significant in a new form.

Soumitra remembers asking Ray about the kind of acting that Bengali cinema needs. Although he had read Stanislavski thanks to Sisir Kumar, it was Ray who gave him his copy of *An Actor Prepares*, the abridged version of the first volume of *An Actor's Work* that had been published in English in the US in 1936. (One of the interesting quirks surrounding this translation gave rise to a general misunderstanding of Stanislavski's 'method'. *An Actor's Work* was divided into three volumes, each detailing one aspect of the process. The first volume concentrated on psychological preparation, the second on body language, and the third on the rehearsal process. A heavily abridged version of just the first volume came out in America as *An Actor Prepares* in 1936, leading the English-speaking world to confuse just the psychological groundwork with the entire 'method' of which it was just a part.) Ray also took him to see Billy Wilder's *The Lost Weekend* at Basusree Cinema. Wilder's

Japanese film poster of *Apur Sansar*

Photo courtesy of Ray Society

unflinching look at alcoholism had Ray Milland in his greatest performance as the inveterate drunkard, Don Birnam. Ray asked Soumitra to observe Milland's performance very closely because in his opinion it offered a comprehensive tutorial for acting in cinema. Oddly enough, Ray Milland did not belong to the new breed of realistic actors. He was a traditional leading man who was at one time the highest paid actor at Paramount Pictures. He acted in Wilder's film to establish his credentials as a dramatic actor. He prepared vigorously, both mentally and physically, and immersed himself in his character to such an extent that he put considerable strain on his home life while the filming went on. He was eventually awarded an Academy Award for his hard work. Though Wilder's treatment of alcoholism is a little tame for modern viewers, Milland's performance is a landmark in acting in American cinema. Ray, who had a scholar's knowledge of American cinema, wanted Soumitra to see the dedication required to build an effective performance.

Eventually Soumitra looked upon his mentor in the same way that he looked upon the professors he admired in college and, of course, Sisir Kumar Bhaduri.

He was the ardent disciple, and nowhere was this more evident than in a story he recalls during the making of *Apur Sansar*. He and Ray, along with the rest of the crew, were on their way to Netarhat, where they would shoot the scenes of Apu wandering desolate after the death of his wife. They had taken the train from Howrah to Muri, where they would have to change trains to go to Ranchi. Soumitra kept asking Ray questions as he was wont to do, and Ray patiently explained the mechanics of the cinematic art. He learnt how film is really just another language, that has its own grammar and its very own syntax. It has its narrative techniques just like literature does, and it is capable of telling the profoundest story provided one understands how the language works. That night forever changed how Soumitra looked at cinema. Decades later in 1986 he made a documentary to memorialise Rabindranath Tagore's 125th birth anniversary called *Stree Ka Patra*. He had already acted in 125 films by then, but he realised that if not for that one night with the master, he would have been all at sea while making the documentary.

Poster of *Charulata* (1964)

Photo courtesy of Ray Society

EARLY YEARS WITH THE MASTER

Apur Sansar was swiftly followed by roles in Ray's next two films – as Umaprasad in *Devi* (1960) and as Amulya in *Samapti* (the last episode of the trilogy known as *Teen Kanya* released in 1961). In *Devi*, Ray attacked superstition. Umaprasad was a supporting role, because the film really belonged to Sharmila Tagore. *Samapti*, a short film lasting no more than 68 minutes, marked the debut of Aparna Sen. In it Soumitra played the delightfully awkward and pompous Amulya. It was an important film for Ray because it was his first adaptation of Tagore. He changed the character's name from Apurva to Amulya in order to avoid confusion with Apurva Roy in *Apur Sansar*. The film is really about Mrinmoyee's (played by Aparna) coming of age, maturing from rebellious tomboy to a sensitive, caring woman. Yet Soumitra plays Amulya with such comic aplomb that he is memorable right through. His growing understanding of his craft is reflected in the amount of depth he is able to instil in this character.

In a particular sequence, Amulya goes to see a prospective bride. He is very self-conscious, stiff, and takes himself extremely seriously. He keeps a portrait of Napoleon on his shelf, its incongruity in the rustic village underlining his pretentiousness. The father of the bride, unctuous and incessantly giggling (played hilariously by Santosh Dutta) sits beside him. Amulya, surrounded by staring children and relatives, tries to initiate conversation with the young woman who is absolutely still and silent except for when she is galvanised into robotic action through judicious prodding by an elderly relative. Everything is

Soumitra shooting for *Samapti* (1961) with Satyajit Ray and Aparna Sen
Photo courtesy of Ray Society

played for laughs and Soumitra's Amulya is shy, awkward, pretentious and clearly uncomfortable. It was a marked departure from the roles he had played, and it was quite apparent that he had comic timing in droves if the occasion called for it.

Yet, there is more to his performance than comic timing alone. He brings a measure of sensitivity and compassion to it that stops Amulya from being nothing more than a caricature. When Mrinmoyee in her rage at being locked in a room throws his books all around, he breaks down at the sight of his favourite books strewn all over the floor. It was a difficult balancing act, and it shows a rare degree of control for an actor that early in his career. Soumitra, guided by Ray's deft handling, created a pitch-perfect character whose reality

Soumitra in his first comic role being filmed by Satyajit Ray in *Samapti* (1961)
Photo courtesy of Ray Society

is not compromised by buffoonery, but is rather expressed through a comic perspective. Amulya is somewhat supercilious, and rather full of himself, but he is never unsympathetic or a simple parody. He has an arc of his own, and at the end seems a more responsible man than he had been at the beginning. Soumitra, who had a lot of fun doing the role, saw himself as any other Bengali youth who at some time or the other has either been painfully self-conscious or taken himself much too seriously.

Samapti was hailed as the best of the acclaimed trilogy, and Soumitra was exemplary in it. Shyam Benegal had nothing but praise for his performance. He spoke at length about its subtle nuances and the considerable skill and craft that had gone into it. Benegal noted that Soumitra had made it look simple,

A still from *Samapti* (1961)
Photo courtesy of Ray Society

even though a lot of effort must have gone into the performance itself. He compared it to an exquisite Persian carpet, and said that it is only when you turn it over that you notice the complicated and elaborate weaving that had produced the seamless beauty on the other side.

Whether it was by accident or because he had been taken in by Ray at such an early age, Soumitra escaped being typecast from the very beginning of his career. He had played a character that invited mockery in only his fourth film, which no one wishing to be a star would ever have done.

Even though he was conventionally handsome, Soumitra never thought he was particularly photogenic. He chose to trust the person doing his make-up and his cinematographer and director to take care of how he looked on screen. He admits that it prevented him from obsessing over his appearance on screen. He could give his entire attention to creating an effective character.

The purposeful seriousness of both Sisir Kumar and Ray no doubt fostered this attitude in him. He could not remain true to his own notions of what cinema and acting should be if he started worrying about stardom. It would have made him a bit of a hypocrite and perhaps would have cut short his long partnership with Ray.

Since he was intent on giving each character the individuality it deserved, he consciously avoided developing mannerisms or gestures that would repeat themselves no matter who he is playing. He developed the art of self-effacement, moulding himself into the character until the audience would be tricked into thinking that they were watching the character and not Soumitra, the actor.

It is perhaps his greatest achievement that when one thinks of the career of Soumitra, one does not think of any particular persona with a distinct style of delivery and mannerisms. One can only recall memories of all the people he has so successfully brought to life over the course of a long career.

Soumitra's flexibility was perhaps never more tested than when he played the illiterate, hot-tempered Narsingh in Ray's *Abhijaan* (1962). Narsingh was so very different from who he was that it constituted one of the biggest challenges of his career. He himself is rather proud of his performance, and counts it among his favourites. He had already worked in Tapan Sinha's *Kshudhita Pashan* in 1960, and his confidence was on the ascendant. His portrayal of Narsingh was so outside his comfort zone, that it established his chameleon-like talent once and for all.

Interestingly enough, neither he nor Ray were initially associated with the film. Ray's *Kanchenjunga* that had come out earlier that year had been a box office failure, and it had left him a little on edge. Ray had written the screenplay for *Abhijaan* from Tarashankar Bandyopadhyay's short story of the same name for Bijoy Chatterjee, who was trying to make a commercially successful film. Bijoy had wanted Uttam Kumar to play the protagonist. When talks fell through, Bijoy approached Soumitra who readily agreed.

Ray who had never written a screenplay that he had not directed was a little apprehensive about how it would be handled. When Bijoy asked him to visit the studio on the first day of shooting, Ray soon took over proceedings. It is possible that Bijoy, who was simply trying to make a neat profit, felt nervous at the prospect of helming a complex script like this one. Soumitra recalls how the outdoor shoot at Birbhum was cancelled at the last minute. Soon

Soumitra as Narsingh, one of his most successful attempts at playing against type in *Abhijaan* (1962)
Photo courtesy of Ray Society

after, when he met Ray, he said that he was being asked to take over as director. Soumitra, sensing another opportunity to work with him, encouraged him to take it up. Ray did and when the film came out, it attracted some criticism because some critics thought it was much too melodramatic for Ray. Soumitra's portrayal of Narsingh also divided the critics.

Abhijaan was from the beginning a bit of an oddity. It was meant for the reigning superstar at the time, and probably would have been a very different film if Bijoy Chatterjee had seen it through. Ray who stayed away from big stars all through his career unless his script demanded their presence, would also have to work with Waheeda Rehman, one of the biggest names in the Hindi film industry. Soumitra, the poster boy for the genteel, educated, sensitive Bengali middle class would have to play Narsingh, a brooding, coarse, illiterate Rajput taxi driver with a violent temper. In spite of all this,

Soumitra worked very hard to change his appearance and mannerisms to play Narsingh in *Abhijaan* (1962)
Photo courtesy of Ray Society

Abhijaan was along with *Goopy Gyne Bagha Byne*, Ray's most commercially successful films.

When the film released, Soumitra's portrayal seemed unconvincing to some critics, who were not at all prepared for such a startling departure from what he had done before. They found his beard and wig unrealistic and the general consensus among the naysayers was that Soumitra had been terribly miscast, and that this was a rare false step for Ray.

There is some truth to these criticisms, because the make-up was inconsistent at times, and the wig and beard less than convincing. These were not small hurdles when you consider how his physical alteration played a significant role in creating the character. The schedule was punishing, and he would have to sit for make-up for two hours twice a day. The heat at Dubrajpur, Birbhum, was so unbearable that shooting could only happen before 10:30

in the morning and after 2:30 in the afternoon. In spite of all this Soumitra's portrayal was of astonishing range and verisimilitude.

Later Soumitra would recall how nervous he was during the whole shoot. Everyone apart from Robi Ghosh was senior to him. According to him, it was one of those rare films in which everyone acted superbly. He was under a fair bit of pressure to deliver a difficult character in these circumstances. He prepared for it by recalling all the times he had spent fraternising with bus conductors and drivers as well as taxi drivers, when he was growing up in Howrah.

He needed to get the physicality of the man right, and he brought a certain menacing defiance to Narsingh's body language. He figured that his pride in his Rajput ancestry as well as his temper would make him a physically aggressive man. He would then have to erase all signs of gentility, urban polish and education from his features. The make-up, which in any case was inadequate, could only do so much.

Soumitra developed a Bengali-English patois for the character. He had heard taxi drivers in Calcutta use it and he suggested to Ray that it would sound more authentic. He also used his expressive eyes to good effect. He erased the gentle refinement in them, and replaced it with an ill-bred hostility which remained his baseline expression except when he talked to Neeli (played by Ruma Guha Thakurta). His awkward advances towards her, so very unlike Apu's poetic exuberance, and his glowering suspicion at everything else are examples of his increasing grasp of his craft. He also spent a lot of time driving the Chrysler used in the film, so that he did not look like an amateur. While rehearsing in Calcutta with Robi Ghosh, he was driving a little too fast and almost hit a man. Visibly shaken, the man turned around and shouted, 'You bloody son of a Punjabi!' Soumitra considered it high praise because the man on the street had mistaken him for an illiterate Hindi-speaking taxi driver.

In *Abhijaan*, Soumitra went against type and portrayed an unattractive person in every sense of the term. This uncompromising dedication to the truth of the character made him a very new kind of actor in Bengali cinema.

In his next film with Ray he went back to his roots. In the 1964 film *Charulata* he played Amal, a character very reminiscent of Apu except the story is told from the perspective of the eponymous protagonist played by Madhabi Mukherjee. *Charulata*, an adaptation of Tagore's *Nashtaneer*, is one of Ray's most critically acclaimed works, especially in the west where it was hailed as his masterpiece. Later Ray wondered whether the western audience truly appreciated the inherently Bengali character of the film, details and elements that only a native viewer could truly grasp.

It also led to some controversy because Ray had deviated considerably from his source material, and any departure from Tagore was considered sacrilegious. Perhaps the biggest divergence was the shift in perspective. Tagore's story about the undoing of a relationship is seen from the point of view of Bhupati, whose steady downfall reaches a climactic point of despondency when he finds out that his wife was in love with someone else. Bhupati, defined by his anglophilia and somewhat stuffy and pompous demeanour despite being idealistic, progressive and well meaning, is a very different character from what is portrayed by Sailen Mukherjee in the film. Ray insisted that his film was an interpretation of *Nashtaneer* told from the point of view of the woman, which he explained was why he changed the name. *Nashtaneer* also had autobiographical elements because Tagore had modelled Amal on his own young self. And so when the importance of the character grew in the film version, it was a foregone conclusion that Soumitra would play a fictional version of Tagore in it.

The growing attraction between the intelligent but deeply neglected and sheltered Charulata and Amal, her brother-in-law, sees Ray at his most lyrical. Amal, who comes into her life during a violent storm, is meant to play a functional role.

Soumitra injected such restless enthusiasm and ebullience into the role that it is not difficult to understand why he (compared to her staid and serious husband) sweeps young Charu off her feet. Amal basks in the attention of his pretty and accomplished sister-in-law, while she falls in love with him. Amal, who has a deep regard and affection for Charu's husband, leaves long before the famous last freeze frame that leaves the future undetermined for Bhupati and Charulata.

Amal's youthful romanticism and love for poetry made Soumitra ideal for the role. His portrayal of Apu and Amulya had probably made it a kind of default mode for him. However, while Ray's reorientation of the source material had given greater importance to Amal, he was still a functional character who does not really have an arc of his own. He unwittingly causes great damage and, distressed at what he has done, he leaves as suddenly as he had come.

In spite of this, Soumitra went through a period of intensive preparation for the role. There are several scenes in the film in which we are shown Amal writing poetry. Soumitra's natural penmanship was rounded, a style that had in fact been developed by Tagore himself. Ray thought that it would be rather unrealistic if he wrote like that during that era. He asked Soumitra to change his handwriting to reflect the prevailing pre-Tagore styles. He remembers that it took him six months of dedicated practice. He wrote diaries, and copied from whatever was available until he had changed his penmanship entirely. In fact, he was so successful that it became permanent. Whenever after that Ray saw anything he had written, he would with some smugness ask Soumitra if he was not happy that his handwriting had improved so much thanks to him. Soumitra chose a higher tenor for his voice to suit someone barely out of his teens. He made up a detailed background for Amal, following the same technique that had worked so well for Apu.

This hard work paid off because Amal is a fully realised character; one whose natural virtuousness and cheerfulness endeared him to the audience immediately. His lack of guile and his irrepressible exuberance ensured that his relationship with Charu never seemed sordid or sleazy. Soumitra was also careful about playing the young and dreamy-eyed poet Amal differently so that comparisons with Apu did not arise. The popularity of the character has endured, marking it as one of his most fondly remembered roles in the Bengali cultural memory.

In *Abhijaan* and in *Charulata*, Soumitra not only plays a character different in every way from himself but also a variant of a character that had made him famous in the first place.

One of Soumitra's abiding memories of *Charulata* is his conversation with Ray about the ending. The latter had originally wanted it to end with Charu taking a distraught Bhupati by the hand and leading him inside. It would have neither agreed with the source material nor provided a satisfying closure to the story. Ray was not really happy but he had made his peace with it. Soumitra told him that it was not really working, and that the positive ending was a little too facile. Charu and Bhupati are devastated, he insisted, and it does not really come across in the ending. The next day Ray cornered him excitedly and told him that he had changed the ending. He had decided to use a freeze frame which would leave everything open-ended and deliberately ambiguous. Ray in a rare moment of childish excitement exclaimed, 'Now, isn't this much better!' The freeze frame became an instant triumph, and Soumitra thinks that he might have nudged the master in that direction.

Charulata was released on 17 April 1964. Soumitra remembers it vividly because it was his father's birthday as well. He took him for the press show on that day. Less than a month later he passed away. It was a terrible blow, from which he took time to recover. Mohitkumar had not been a distant, authoritarian figure. He was an affectionate father, and his impassioned recital of *Debotar Grash* had been among the first inspirations for a life spent performing for an audience.

Soumitra did not work with Ray for four years after *Kapurush* released in 1965. This was an unusually long gap because they had made six films in the six years since *Apur Sansar*. In 1969, Ray adapted *Aranyer Din Ratri*, Sunil Gangopadhyay's novel of the same name into a film that caused more controversy than any of his films had ever done before. Soumitra played Ashim, another departure from type because for the most part he is a fairly unlikeable character. He is a young corporate honcho, confident to the point of arrogance, and has all the barely concealed urban contempt for everything he considers rural and backward. The film which was greatly praised by the foreign media and castigated in Bengal and India is now considered one of the master's greatest works. Its literary structure, subtle and layered characterisation and a mordant critique of the Bengali urban middle class make it one of Ray's

Soumitra and Madhabi Mukherjee in *Charulata* (1964)
Photo courtesy of Ray Society

Soumitra delivered one of his most popular performances in *Charulata* (1964)
Photo courtesy of Ray Society

Above left: English language poster of *Charulata* (1964)
Photo courtesy of Ray Society
Above right: Poster of *Kapurush* (1965)
Photo courtesy of Ray Society

most popular and enduring works. Soumitra as Ashim led an ensemble cast comprising Robi Ghosh, Shubhendu Chatterjee and Shamit Bhanja as a group of friends who have come from the city to the forests of Palamau for a vacation. Sharmila Tagore plays Aparna, a character on whom falls the responsibility of schooling these delusional individuals like a character in a G.B. Shaw play. Aparna Sen had a cameo playing the girl who dumps Hari (Shamit Bhanja) and sends his fragile masculinity into a downward spiral of shame and self-hatred.

The most surprising bit of casting was that of Simi Garewal as the Santhal Duli. Garewal, the very embodiment of suave and anglicised cosmopolitanism, was the last person you would think of for a role of a Santhal woman. Yet, under Ray's direction, she fit the role well, using her innate confidence to very convincingly portray the self-assured sensuality of a Santhal. It is a little difficult to fully appraise Soumitra's performance without taking a close look at the director's thematic intentions.

Sunil Gangopadhyay never particularly liked what Ray had done with his novel. He would later say that it had become a fundamentally different story in the film. The four friends are significantly poorer than their counterparts in the film, and all except one was unemployed. The characters were dissatisfied rebels, radical in their ideas, and there certainly was not any romantic angle anywhere. While Gangopadhyay could be forgiven for being a little tetchy at Ray playing fast and loose with his material, the intelligentsia hastily decided that the director was in his choice of subject being socially irresponsible and perhaps escapist.

Their primary criticism against it was that it ignored the political and social turmoil that had engulfed Bengal at the time. The factious cross currents of discontent that had been simmering under the surface in Calcutta since the mid 1960s finally came to a boil at the end of the decade as the state and its capital caught in the throes of Naxalite uprising descended into utter chaos. The CPI(M), which was the more revolutionary version of the CPI, had brought the city to a complete standstill with strikes everywhere. It was an era when to be a responsible and educated individual was to be deeply political. In Bengal everyone has always generally been in agreement that an artist choosing to be apolitical in such times is running away from reality and therefore not worth anyone's attention.

This of course arose from the fact that Ray's artistic proclivities (unlike his contemporary Ritwik Ghatak) were never particularly wired for turning political events into cinema. He was not detached from the reality of his time, even though he preferred to look through his experiences with a fine-toothed comb to find what appealed to him as a filmmaker. In fact, it is with his Feluda films that he successfully escaped from the political turbulence of his era. *Aranyer Din Ratri* far from being escapist was a brutal takedown of the elitist class-consciousness of an urban middle class whose post-colonial pretensions were as hollow as they were reprehensible. Pauline Kael called it 'perhaps the subtlest, most plangent study of the cultural tragedy of imperialism the screen has ever had'!

The friends quite often use their knowledge of English to comment condescendingly on everything around them, and yet when they run into a group of people who belong to a more sophisticated (read greater command of English) higher class, they are immediately subservient and ingratiatingly polite. These individuals are the inheritors of a western tradition that they try to appropriate in awkward ways to create an identity for themselves that cuts them off from the vast majority of their own countrymen. Ray explores the inconsistencies and fallacies in these identities by taking them out of their urban milieu in the film.

Soumitra's Ashim works in a company and is doing fairly well for himself. He is smug and confident, and his very urban assumptions of superiority are obnoxious. Sharmila recalls how she found Ashim to be quite repugnant, and the only thing that redeems him is that he understands his flaws and by the end of the film is a better man for it.

When Ashim sees Santhals dancing, he glibly calls it the 'Santhal twist'. It is offensive on several counts and exposes how difficult it is for him to interpret anything without running it through his pseudo-western perspective. Early in the film he bribes the hapless caretaker so that they can stay in the guesthouse even though they have not taken the requisite official permissions. He does so with haughty arrogance, and with the air of one who knows that in this conflict, such as it is, he holds all the power.

The character was a particularly challenging one to pull off for him. It was overlaid with layers of subtle social and historical commentary. Ashim was as much a representative figure as Apu once was more than a decade back. What is more, it was a complex character that owing to its strong arc defied any attempt to classify it as negative or positive. Looking back, Soumitra says that he was lucky that these intellectually alert and gifted directors gave him the opportunities to portray characters of such lasting quality and relevance. Ashim certainly was not easy to play. While the polite self-deprecation of the cultured '*bhadrolok*' came pretty easily to him by then, the brittle conceit of hollow posturing was something new. Soumitra employed an understated swagger, different from the more obvious one he had used for Mayurbahan in *Jhinder Bondi*. He is cocksure, haughty to those he considers social inferiors and deferential to those he considers above him in the social hierarchy.

Ray helped him understand that it was all a façade, and not a particularly strong one, because there are no solid principles and beliefs underpinning it. Consequently, there is an undertone of vulnerability in his confident demeanour. This is exposed when Aparna snubs him repeatedly. Soumitra straddles this fine line really well, the subtle play of expressions on his expressive face running the gamut of emotions from superciliousness to doubt and humiliation. When at the end, he returns to the city, he is a wiser man with greater self-awareness. There is now a modicum of humility in his general demeanour.

He spent a lot of time with his co-stars, which added to the sense of companionship that we see among them in the film. He remembers discussing a scene at the tavern where they would have to get very drunk with Robi Ghosh. The latter told him that he should add a few drunken coughs during the performance. It ended up adding to the authenticity of his drunken act.

Soumitra has nothing but pleasant memories of the shoot. They would go off on jaunts to the nearby tribal village. Ray would never join them but would fix them with a mock-serious stare at breakfast the next day and ask sternly, 'So when did you return last night?'

The weather was quite hot and everyone slept outside on cots even though Ray would never venture out of his room at night. Soumitra who shared a bungalow with him recalls how dismayed he was when he found out that he had forgotten to pack his pyjamas. Soumitra offered him one of his lungis but Ray would have none of it. He decided to wear his trousers to bed but the weather was stifling and Soumitra found himself woken up one night by an abashed Ray asking for the lungi. 'How do you even wear this?' he grumbled.

Soumitra and Sharmila Tagore in *Aranyer Din Ratri* (1970)
Photo courtesy of Ray Society

The next morning he was sullen and asked Soumitra, 'How do you sleep in that thing?'

Soumitra says that even though he and the rest of the crew would generally be in awe of Ray, he could still surprise them with acts of sheer virtuosity. Something like that happened when they were shooting the 'memory game' sequence in *Aranyer Din Ratri*. The actors sat on the ground in a circle and each person would have to add something to an ever-lengthening list of things for the next person to remember and recite. Ray had placed the camera in the middle and wanted to move from person to person tracking the whole thing in a circular manner. It was a particularly difficult thing to do because it was impossible for anyone to look through the viewfinder while operating it. He did it blind using his judgement to pause at the right place as he moved from one actor to the next. As it turned out, when the footage was replayed for editing, it was clear that he had paused at the right moment each time without any error. Soumitra says that whenever he sees the sequence, he cannot help but marvel at the smooth framing of each actor that would not have been any better even if he were actually looking through the viewfinder.

Thirty-three years after it was released, the celebrated filmmaker Goutam Ghose made a sequel called *Abar Aranye* which had the cast returning to the forest of Palamau except Simi Garewal, and Robi Ghosh who had passed away in 1997. The enduring relevance of these characters made it seem that there were more stories to be told about them, or at least that the stories needed a conclusion. The sequel, even though it has callbacks to the previous film in the form of interspersed footage from the original, seems very different in spirit and tone. Soumitra thought that since the original film had ended without any certainty of Ashim and Aparna getting together, the fact that the sequel began with them being married for a while made it seem like they are very different characters. He did not think that apart from their names, the characters in the sequels had much in common with their older incarnations.

After *Aranyer Din Ratri*, Ray made his trilogy of films on the metropolis, and he did not cast Soumitra in any of them. Soumitra has never held it against him that despite their closeness, he did not use him in even one of them. He had a tremendous respect for his judgement, and simply accepted that he was not right for what Ray was trying to say in those films. Soumitra always treated Ray with all the affectionate deference of a disciple for his guru. His role in his life went far beyond the roles he got in his films, and he thought it churlish to hold grudges about films in which he did not get to act. Besides, Ray would immortalise him in the popular culture of Bengal in a few years when he would offer him the lead in a detective-adventure film called *Sonar Kella*.

FELUDA

Feluda has been portrayed by several actors, and each of them has tried in some way or the other to make the character their own. It is a daunting task because for most Bengalis, Soumitra Chatterjee's portrayal of the detective is the definitive version. Feluda is a character firmly entrenched in the Bengali popular imagination, and inextricably bound with childhood nostalgia to boot. This has ensured that Soumitra's performance apart from its critical value is perhaps more important for the affection and loyalty that it inspires among his people.

A lot can be written about Feluda, mostly because almost every Bengali who has grown up either reading the books or watching the first two Ray classics has memories and experiences associated with the character. When Satyajit Ray revived *Sandesh* (a children's magazine started by his grandfather Upendrakishore Ray Chowdhury in 1913 and revived briefly by his father Sukumar Ray in the 1930s) in 1961, he started writing stories for children and teenagers. His two most popular characters created during this time were the eccentric scientist Professor Shonku and P.C. Mitter or Feluda, the private investigator. These stories were very deliberately aimed at a young demographic, and therefore never dealt with subjects and themes that would be considered inappropriate for them. In a very specific sense, Ray prefigured by several decades the Young Adult genre of popular literature which is so prevalent now.

Both Professor Shonku and Feluda represent different facets of the author himself. There is no doubt that the latter owes much to his literary predecessors, especially Conan Doyle's Sherlock Holmes and Agatha Christie's Hercule Poirot. It is also quite clear that the American hard-boiled tradition played a role in the manner in which some of the stories were structured and executed. Furthermore, there was also the very popular Sharadindu Bandyopadhyay's *Satyanweshi* (seeker of truth) in Bengal to reckon with.

Soumitra says that what attracted him most to the character was his unstinting faith in his intellect as his primary weapon against the wickedness and chaos in the world. In *Joy Baba Felunath*, when the young Captain Spark wants to see his gun, Feluda tells him with his usual conviction that even though he does have one, his brain is far more powerful than any gun. He calls it his '*magojastra*' (brain-weapon).

It was however his quintessential Bengaliness that made him a distinctive figure. He was always in kurta-pyjamas and smoked only Charminar cigarettes. He belonged to the educated urban middle class in word and gesture. He did not have any of the eccentricities of Holmes (addiction to opium would be unacceptable on all possible levels) or the dainty prissiness of Poirot. He is the detective next door, the archetypal *bhadrolok* who is self-effacing and reserved. His encyclopaedic knowledge about things and his penchant for travel gave Ray opportunities to point out interesting factoids and information to his young readers. Feluda is however relentless and absolutely fearless when he takes a case. He has a very strong sense of right and wrong, great compassion for those wronged by others, and is driven by the courage of his convictions.

Soumitra insists that Ray's sketches of the character resemble the author far more than they do him. He adds that he could see so much of Ray in Feluda that it was impossible for him to play him without referencing his creator. He says that those who knew Ray well would immediately recognise his mannerisms and manner of speaking in his performance. In *Sonar Kella*, when Jatayu meets Feluda and Topshe for the first time in the train, he is rattling off heavily accented Hindi in his inimitable fashion. When he realises that there are Bengalis around he is happy to revert to his native language. Feluda tells him that he can continue speaking his Hindi if he wants because he is thoroughly enjoying it. Soumitra had modelled himself on the director to

Poster of *Sonar Kella* (1974)

Photo courtesy of Ray Society

such an extent that he says that if anyone wants to know what Ray talked like, he can do no better than look at him delivering that dialogue. Soumitra was probably being smart about this. Feluda was conceived as an alter ego of the author. Ray had unwittingly or otherwise instilled a lot of himself in him anyway. It was really good sense to try and imitate the creator when the time came to bring the creation to life for the big screen.

Soumitra was an avowed fan of the books much before Ray had any plans to adapt one of them. He was ecstatic when he was offered the role. He was also looking forward to do something his teenage children would like to see.

Feluda did not require a lot of research or the kind of physical and psychological transformation that his other more challenging films demanded. Soumitra says that between the books and the usual meticulous script, there was very little he had to do except follow Ray's directions. While he had read a lot of detective fiction he consciously stayed away from emulating any of them. The shadow of Holmes has always loomed large over fictional detectives that have followed in his footsteps. There was also the hard-boiled American tradition, which in cinema was defined by the fast-talking, tough as nails and cynical Philip Marlowe played definitively by Humphrey Bogart in *The Big Sleep* (1946).

Soumitra actively stayed away from these performances, choosing to approach it like he would approach any other role. He traced his essence to a powerful sense of loyalty, honesty and integrity of purpose and a hyper-intelligent mind. He was also aware that it was not a physically imposing character even though he was strong, knew how to defend himself well and could shoot as well as any of his fictional counterparts. At the end of *Joy Baba Felunath* he corners the heinous Maganlal Meghraj and reduces him to whimpering terror by shooting at the wall around him as punishment for what he had done to Jatayu earlier in the film.

He was nevertheless first and foremost a cerebral hero, and this generally presents a peculiar cinematic problem. Since the exigencies of a detective story require withholding of information, we are never privy to the protagonist's thoughts until the plot demands it. It is never particularly cinematic to show people silently thinking for long stretches of time. Even in the books, Feluda is known to withdraw into sessions of intense silent contemplation. In the films, Ray and Soumitra sought a way around with an ingenious ploy. In *Sonar Kella* when he is deep in thought, he gently drums his furrowed brow with his fingers. It works well, because you can almost see his mind working through the fingers that function as a kind of visual analogue of the act.

Soumitra as Feluda looks at the world with a keen sharpness that gives the audience the impression that he observes everything, as indeed he does. It helps that his assistant is his young nephew (who acts as the surrogate for the intended readership of the books) which gives him the opportunity to teach him all the things he knows without sounding pedantic. Soumitra says that even this was largely taken from Ray. He remembers that Ray had the rare ability to explain the most complex of issues in the simplest of ways. The detective has the same clarity of mind.

Soumitra was careful to not make the character eccentric despite being intellectually gifted. Even his moments of deductive brilliance are understated. Unlike the bipolar, opium addict Holmes who is decidedly cut off from society and whose superior intellect makes him very impatient of those less remarkable, Soumitra plays Feluda as a fairly typical educated member of the Bengali urban middle class.

This may seem like a simple distinction but it is an important one. The greatest detectives are marked by their quirks. Hercule Poirot is obsessive compulsive about not just his appearance, habits and routine but is easily distressed by lapses from his high standards in others. In the stylised noir world of the hard-boiled novels, someone like Philip Marlowe lives on the fringes, and is characterised by his extreme cynicism, mercenary pessimism and lack of faith in human nature. In the context of detective stories, Feluda is a bit of an anomaly. Ray was no doubt inspired by the ordinariness of Byomkesh Bakshi's personal life, because he even more oddly has a wife, a son, and grows older in the course of the stories. Soumitra brings such easy normality to the role that Feluda seems like any other member of the class he represents.

Soumitra plays off this to great effect in the films. One of his favourite dialogues from *Joy Baba Felunath* (which is his personal favourite of the two

English language poster of *Sonar Kella* (1974)
Photo courtesy of Ray Society

Satyajit Ray directing Soumitra during the shooting of *Sonar Kella* (1974)
Photo courtesy of Ray Society

films) comes after Maganlal Meghraj puts Jatayu through the wringer in a sequence as dangerous as it is hilarious. His helplessness and suppressed anger as the doddering Arjun throws knife after knife at the petrified Jatayu turns to steely determination as he sits on the ghat in the Benares twilight and vows that he will take revenge for it or he would give up being a detective. The actor loved this dialogue because one could see the depth of his affection for his friend. His guilt at having put his friend's life in danger, and the humiliation of his powerlessness overcome him. Soumitra felt that this humanised the detective greatly, and gave an indication of the intensity of his emotions under his generally unflappable surface.

The manner in which he played Feluda also had to do with the kind of films they were. The first film is about a boy who believes that he can remember his past life, and the apparent crime that drives the second film turns out to not be a crime at all. In *Sonar Kella* the paranormal aspect of the story (which is neither affirmed nor dismissed) is soon eclipsed by the imminent threat to the boy's life when he is kidnapped by two con artists played by Amiyanath Burman and Mandar Bose (played by Ajoy Banerjee and Kamu Mukherjee to perfection). While it is good old-fashioned detective work that helps save the day, the story itself is not structured like a clue hunt leading to a final revelation. It is as much an adventure as it is anything else constructed as a race with the villains desperately trying to stay one step ahead. Feluda is able to foil their plans because he never misses a trick. This is Soumitra's greatest triumph. All through the film, he is like a bloodhound pursuing them till he catches them. He later said that he wanted to maintain a certain consistency when it came to his portrayal of the detective. He repeated that it was all in the eyes. He had noticed that people with extraordinary intelligence always have a bright, slightly restless look in their eyes. Feluda never looks like he is not thinking, and his articulate eyes reflect the constant workings of a tireless brain. Soumitra's training had always led him to find referents for his performances from real life. He tried it out and Ray did not say anything, which as Soumitra says was tantamount to approval. He was probably used to insightful creative decisions from him by now.

Joy Baba Felunath was filmed four years later, and Soumitra's biggest challenge was to maintain the same pitch and tenor of performance as in the first film. The only real difference, as he wryly says, is that he had to wear a wig because his hairline had started receding by then. He says that he liked the sequel more because it dealt with smuggling invaluable national artefacts out of the country. At the end, Feluda disguised as the charlatan 'Machchli Baba' confronts the villain Maganlal Meghraj. According to Soumitra, his barely suppressed rage and contempt for those who sell national treasures at the foreign market was an indication of Feluda's strong patriotism. He enjoyed saying those lines thoroughly because he thought that it made the character a truly noble one.

The settings of these films played an important role, as they did in the novels as well. Feluda loves travelling, and the schedules in Rajasthan and Benares were good fun for the actors and the crew. It was not always easy though. Even though each aspect of the production was planned down to the last detail, there were unforeseen problems.

Soumitra maintains that Feluda is actually Satyajit Ray's alter ego
Photo courtesy of Ray Society

There would be huge crowds of people waiting to catch a glimpse of the shooting of *Joy Baba Felunath* (1979) in Benares

Photo courtesy of Ray Society

Soumitra shooting for *Joy Baba Felunath* (1979) with Satyajit Ray and Santosh Dutta in Benares

Photo courtesy of Ray Society

Soumitra shooting for *Sonar Kella* (1974) with Satyajit Ray, Santosh Dutta, Siddartha Chatterjee and Kamu Mukherjee
Photo courtesy of Ray Society

In Benares, large crowds had gathered to watch the shooting on the first day. Ray was not happy because they were everywhere, even peeking out of windows, balconies and terraces to get a glimpse of them. They could not manage a single shot that day. Ray was thinking of changing the location altogether when a group of local Bengalis came to their rescue. They promised him that no one will hang around to disturb them and requested him to go ahead as planned. Ray was quite skeptical at the time, but the next day there was no one around. The director was ecstatic and thanked the local people who had followed through with their promise.

The other incident that Soumitra remembers quite vividly happened during the shooting of *Sonar Kella*. It was the last day of shooting and a substantial part of the climax was yet to be shot. Due to the foggy cold weather, there was a very limited number of good usable hours in a day. Furthermore, both Soumitra and Sailen Mukherjee (the real Dr Hazra) had to board a train in the evening because both were scheduled to appear in a play in Calcutta the next day. He knew that it would take a bit of a miracle to manage what was left in a day. In spite of the fact that he had known Ray for almost fifteen years by then, and had acted in several of his films, he was astounded by what Ray pulled off that day. He says that Ray was like a man possessed, working in a frenzy from one shot to the next without the slightest hint of tiredness. He knew the script and the technical requirements so well that he did not consult his notes even once as he set up shots, filmed them and moved on to the next with remarkable efficiency. He had seen something like this when Ray had very little time to shoot a sequence in the rain while filming *Samapti*. Soumitra says that his enthusiasm and work ethic was infectious and raised the standards of everyone around him who scrambled to desperately keep up.

He never ceased to be amazed at his guru's multifaceted talents. In the Jodhpur Circuit House, Feluda is supposed to look through an inland letter where a changed letter in the signature clues him to the fact that the man they knew as Dr Hazra was an impostor. When Ray was handed the inland letter for the shot, he was irritated that someone had forgotten to get the stamp. Too much of a stickler to let it pass, he proceeded to draw a postage stamp on it with such accuracy that it was almost impossible to know the difference at a glance. Soumitra remembers how it looked a little crooked, slightly frayed at the edges as real stamps did, and was the right size and shape even though he was drawing from memory.

Oddly enough, the scene that frightens us the most in *Sonar Kella* was slightly harrowing for the actor as well. Mandar Bose releases a scorpion in Feluda's room and when Soumitra lies down on his bed, the audience realises to their horror that the scorpion is on the bed, only inches away. The scene was shot in Calcutta and, apparently, at that fateful moment when the scorpion was on the bed with him, the lights went out. Soumitra recalled that there was very little to do but lie quietly and wait for the lights to come back on. He felt strangely calm, and had resigned himself to the terrible pain of a scorpion sting, when the lights came back on. Mercifully, the scorpion had decided to make its way down to the floor where it was captured soon after.

Soumitra's stardom received a tremendous boost with Feluda. He would be mobbed on the roads by legions of adoring fans. Soon it became quite clear that in the public imagination, he would perhaps be mostly remembered for playing the detective. He says that in those early days this did not sit well with him. He found it a little stifling. He was also somewhat resentful of the fact that his other characters that required a lot more work, like Gangacharan in *Ashani Sanket*, were not as popular. This eventually changed when he learnt to accept that he could not really control which character the masses would choose to remember him as the most. He later wrote that even if one person remembers him for any character he has played he should consider himself lucky.

These two films were not his only outings as Feluda. He voiced the character in two radio plays based on *Baksho Rahasya* and *Gosainpur Sargaram*. Ray's son Sandip Ray who carries on the legacy of Feluda on screen now, wrote the scripts. Soumitra returned to play the sleuth in the early 1990s when two of the novels *Ghurghutiyar Ghotona and Golokdham Rahasya*, were adapted for Doordarshan by Bibhas Chakraborty. Soumitra who was in his fifties then was quite reluctant to play the role again but could not back down after Ray requested him to do it. He thinks that it is important that Feluda be a young man because he is someone the kids look up to.

The role has passed on to other actors, and Soumitra is all praise for them. Feluda is quite simply Bengal's only extremely successful film franchise and is probably one of the very rare properties in the industry that ensure a good return at the box office on the strength of its reputation alone. He thinks Sabyasachi Chakrabarty was very good, and matured into the role nicely. He always thought that any actor who takes on the role of Feluda has to be able to use his eyes well, and Sabyasachi learnt to do that quite effectively. He is very happy that the baton has passed to Abir Chatterjee (who has also played Byomkesh Bakshi in a number of films). He has the talent and physicality to play Feluda well, he says. Soumitra adds that even more importantly he is the right age to play him.

LAST YEARS WITH THE MASTER

Ashani Sanket took Ray away from the city (his last few films had all been on life in the big city) and gave Soumitra one of the most significant acting challenges in his career. Satyajit Ray's biographer Andrew Robinson said that the director had wanted to make a film on the disastrous famine of 1943 ever since the mid-1960s. Soumitra himself was very keen to take on the role of Gangacharan, the village Brahmin whose life is turned upside down by the famine. He prepared harder for this role than for any other in his life, and it helped him to deliver one of the strongest performances in his career.

This role was personally important for Soumitra because he still vividly remembered the suffering and death the famine had caused all around him in Krishnanagar. It helped that the setting of the film was a village in Nadia (Krishnanagar is part of the Nadia district). He went along with Ray while he went location hunting and saw the people there very closely. They went to several villages, and Soumitra fell back on his natural training as he closely observed the way the Brahmins carried themselves, their way of squatting on the ground, the general almost absent-minded habit of touching the *poite*. Ray used to joke that he should really make *Ashani Sanket* soon considering they had someone who looked so much like a Brahmin. Yet, there was need for preparation. He had taken up this project because it seemed to him of some serious social significance. He was going to portray a character caught in the midst of one of the worst calamities in the history of Bengal. What was more important was that it affected the poor in the villages much more than

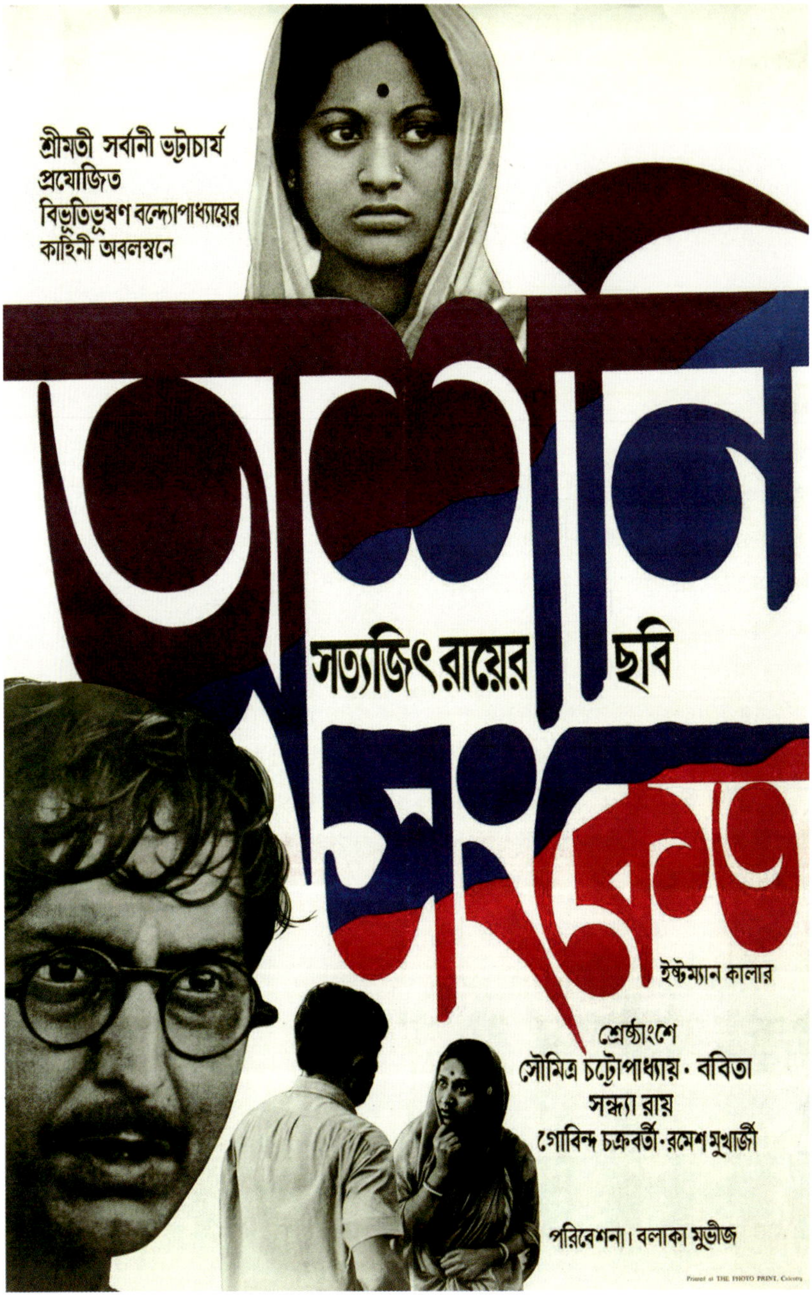

Poster of *Ashani Sanket* (1973)
Photo courtesy of Ray Society

Ray sketching a profile of Soumitra for *Ashani Sanket* (1973)
Photo courtesy of Ray Society

it did the ones living in Calcutta. Ray who remembered not being especially concerned during those years when he was working for an advertising agency in Calcutta no doubt felt a little guilty about it, and this was his way of making amends for it. Soumitra with his strong leftist leanings found the subject to be really important. This in turn put greater responsibility on him to deliver a really good performance.

Soumitra later recalled how it was a learning experience in more ways than one. He had always identified himself as a true Bengali and a son of the soil. However, the time spent exploring and shooting in these rural settings made it very clear that there was a wide disconnect between him (and anyone else who belonged to the city) and the rural heartland of the country. It disappointed him that his outlook and way of life was much too urban and westernised for him to fully identify with what he saw around him. It was a rude shock and dejected him somewhat.

It probably propelled him to put in a lot of hard work while shooting. He wrote copious notes on the character, a practice that had held him in good stead ever since those green fledgling days when he had played Apu. He created the character from the foundation, keeping a record of his education, the subjects he would be teaching at his *paathshala*, and the kind of medicinal advice (Ayurveda or homeopathy) he would be dispensing to the villagers. He looked upon his preparation as a work in progress, and he says that it was really only on the last day of shooting that he thought he was well prepared to perform the role.

Gangacharan is both a type and a complex individual who goes through an extremely steep learning curve in the course of the film. He is the only Brahmin in the village, and by virtue of that alone a well-respected figure. The foreign press spoke at length of the slow, subdued plot that spends a lot of time establishing the regular patterns and rhythms of village life before Ray shows its complete breakdown under the stress of starvation and suffering. They praised Soumitra's performance because it showed not just a greater range but also his consistency and masterful control of his craft. And while it does show him at the pinnacle of his abilities, the performance can only be really understood in its context.

Gangacharan's easy assumption of superiority can only be appreciated if one knows of the position of a Brahmin in a village. He is not only the most educated man in the village, but he is also their indisputable social superior. He

Ray's sketch of Soumitra as Gangacharan in *Ashani Sanket* (1973)
Photo courtesy of Ray Society

is the repository of all spiritual knowledge and the trusted intermediary between man and whichever god needs propitiating at any given point. Gangacharan is clever and knows how to take advantage of the great deference with which he is treated. He is not very well educated in the strictest sense. He knows the Japanese have taken Singapore even though he has not the slightest idea where Singapore is. He leverages it to make as much money as he can by acting as a teacher, priest and doctor. One of the cornerstones of his character is established when he is invited by someone from the next village to do a *pujo* to rid them of a cholera epidemic. He does the *pujo* diligently and then also gives them sound scientific advice on how to deal with the disease.

Gangacharan's clever manipulation of his fellow villagers never descends into naked avarice or wicked exploitation. It is largely what a man of his caste in such a situation would be expected to do in any case. This is what allows him

Soumitra as Gangacharan in *Ashani Sanket* (1973)
Photo courtesy of Ray Society

to be both an individual and a representative figure. Ray builds up the impact of food shortage with studied deliberation until the rising desperation explodes in violence. Soumitra tries to stop a couple of men from beating a thief up and is shoved aside and abused. Sprawled on the ground, his dignity shattered, Gangacharan looks on in shocked terror as his world comes crashing down in that instant. This is the hinge the plot turns on, and Soumitra's look of sudden fright indicates not just the desperation of the situation but foreshadows the catastrophic breakdown of an ancient hierarchical social structure. By the end, when he attends the dying 'untouchable' woman and then gives her a proper burial, he has flouted all the extremely rigid rules of his caste. The social construct from which he had derived his identity through tradition has been

Listening intently to the Master

Photo courtesy of Ray Society

destroyed, and it forces him to find his own humanity. He does so at the end when he serenely looks at the great number of people he will have to feed.

Ray's script uses a representative village to faithfully record the devastation caused by the famine – suffering, death, and total social collapse. It also acts as the backdrop to a redemptive character arc for the protagonist. Gangacharan learns to abandon his cherished privileges and acquires a measure of compassion and wisdom by the end.

Soumitra's research allowed him to inhabit the skin of the character in a way rarely replicated in Indian cinema. His slightly smug complacency, his fondness for the small indulgences of life, and his confident, starchy appearance (complete with a prim little moustache) at the beginning of the film quickly establishes Gangacharan as an extremely believable character – the kind you would have recognised immediately in any of the villages in Bengal. Soumitra had reservations about the moustache because he did not think that Brahmins had them at the time. Ray agreed but insisted on this bit of anachronism. His face was an easily recognisable one and had certain associations too because of his stardom. The wispy little moustache changed his face enough to differentiate him from how he looked in commercial cinema. Soumitra got a period-appropriate set of glasses as well from Chakraberia Hawkers' Corner. The combination of the moustache and the glasses along with his astute understanding of body language went a long way in creating verisimilitude of character.

Gangacharan's arc in the film moves from terrible disillusionment to an assertion of empathy and humanism. The journey is expertly tracked by Ray, and Soumitra unleashes a wide repertoire of techniques to capture every subtle and obvious shift along the way. At the end, as he stands near his gate looking down the pathway at a group of people coming towards him in the grimy, yellow dawn, the privations of the famine and the turmoil have changed him. He looks apprehensive but there is empathy in his eyes now. There is calm acceptance in his tone making it clear that he is a different man.

Considering the challenges of physicality and language, along with the complexity of the character and the journey it undertakes, Gangacharan was

Soumitra in a still from *Hirak Rajar Deshe* (1980)
Photo courtesy of Ray Society

among the most challenging roles of Soumitra's career. The film itself is deceptive in its low-key, understated treatment of its subject. Ray probably thought that the subject matter was poignant and tragic enough and did not need cinematic emphasis to underscore its pathos. The sweep of the devastation in which the collapse of order in the village is almost a synecdoche for the desolation all over Bengal gives the story an almost epic grandeur. Soumitra's Gangacharan stands right in the middle of it, his journey echoing the awful loss of life and suffering of millions of people. The protagonist, an everyman figure like any other, acquires epic resonance because he goes through an experience that completely uproots his world leaving him to reconstruct an identity in an unrecognisable world. Soumitra plays Gangacharan with tremendous sympathy and authenticity, ensuring that he is the medium through whom the audience understands what he himself remembered of those terrible years when famine ravaged Bengal.

Soumitra and Dhritiman Chatterjee in *Ganashatru* (1990)
Photo courtesy of Ray Society

In the 1980s Ray's health started deteriorating starting with a heart attack in October 1983. He was shooting *Ghare-Baire* at the time, which got delayed. He recovered but was not allowed by his doctors to make films for a while. Soumitra who remembers being very distressed at his mentor's ill health would often visit him at his Bishop Lefroy road residence. He says that it was upsetting to see Ray cooped up at home because it was for all intents and purposes a form of imprisonment for a workaholic like him. Even when he was given permission to resume work, there were stringent conditions. For the rest of his career he would only make films that did not require him to move out of the studio too much. Soumitra acted in all of them except *Agantuk*, his last film.

Poster of *Ghare-Baire* (1984)
Photo courtesy of Ray Society

Ray managed to finish *Ghaire-Baire* by deputising his son Sandip Ray to complete the project under his directions. Soumitra's role as Sandip proved to be a divisive one, with critics not sure whether it was a tour de force or an uneven and a slightly underwhelming performance.

It was a bold experiment in any case. Soumitra was yet again playing against type as a smooth-talking, charming but unscrupulous man who does not think twice before seducing his friend's wife to get his money. It was much more of a challenge than his last major role in a Ray film, Dr Ashok Gupta in *Ganashatru* (1990). It was an adaptation of Henrik Ibsen's *An Enemy of the People* in which he plays the beleaguered protagonist desperately holding on to the truth despite the rising tide of hatred against him. Playing a decent, principled man battling society and choosing integrity over convenience was by then a 'bread-and-butter' role for him. He essays it with great sincerity and quiet determination. It is nevertheless Sandip in *Ghare-Baire* that is his last great role in a Ray film.

Much like with *Ashani Sanket*, Ray had always wanted to make *Ghare-Baire*. It kept on getting delayed mostly because Ray was never happy with the actors who would portray the other two characters in the triangle. He had thought of Madhabi Mukherjee and even the reigning box office queen Suchitra Sen but it never worked out. Ray was an astute student of Tagore and he knew that Bimala in the novel was never supposed to be very good looking. Therefore it would not have made sense to cast conventionally beautiful actresses to play the role. He eventually cast Swatilekha Chatterjee whom he had seen performing on stage in 1981, and had liked her proficiency in Bengali.

Ray had initially wanted Soumitra to play the character of Nikhilesh, the idealistic, compassionate zamindar. However, over the years, as he became less and less sure about finding the right actor for the manipulative and cunning radical Sandip, he decided that if he finds someone right for either role, Soumitra would have to play the other one. It was as good a measure of Ray's confidence in the actor as any that he believed it was possible for him to play both characters that were conceived as symbols of diametrically opposite ideologies. Eventually, he cast the delicate-featured Victor Banerjee as Nikhil and the villainous role of Sandip went to Soumitra.

When *Ghare-Baire* was released it received a mixed national reception at best (despite getting its usual share of accolades from Ray loyalists in the foreign press). Unfortunately, following on the heels of Ray's illness, the film came to be associated as the first of his last films that did not quite match up to the quality of his earlier work. It was unfairly compared to *Charulata* with which it bore more than a few superficial similarities. Unusually for a Ray film, the performances came in for a bit of stick as well. Soumitra was criticised for lacking sufficient flair and not convincing enough as a devious amoral man.

It may have been misplaced though, because Soumitra brings his usual sincerity and preparation to Sandip as well. He had played negative roles before – with flair and panache as Mayurbahan – but there is something fairly repulsive about the manipulative selfishness and moral cowardice that lurks beneath the smooth, charming and eloquent exterior of Sandip. He is also a very effective orator, which made Ray's decision to give the role to Soumitra that much easier. Ray had always admired the clarity of his diction and his way with the language. It was one of the primary reasons that he had cast him as Apu to begin with. Soumitra was well suited to give a good account of himself while working with a director who prioritised fluency in Bengali over a lot of other conventional qualities.

Soumitra was asked to memorise an entire speech which he was supposed to deliver at one go because Ray had told him that there would only be one take. He later found out that it was eventually edited in order to accommodate Bimala's reactions. He brought his childhood memories of freedom fighters delivering orations into play, and effectively mimicked their body language and heightened dramatic delivery. He had to be charming at first considering that it would take a lot for a woman of Bimala's social station at that time to cheat on her husband. In his initial interactions with her he is amiable, passionate and, in his pleasant face, there is no sign of any deception. As the film progresses, this changes considerably, which in turn suggests that there is a clearly defined arc for his character.

As his true motives become clear there is a greater degree of furtiveness and cunning in him. He is vulnerable and adoring when he wants to seduce Bimala, yet at moments when his self-interest is threatened, there is a glimmer of ruthlessness in his expression. Midway through the film, Nikhilesh confronts Sandip and tells him that he will not tolerate harassment (imposition of *swadeshi* on those who cannot afford it) of his Muslim subjects. Sandip tells him that the Muslim population all over the country is falling in with the idea of *swadeshi*. Nikhilesh retorts by reminding him that they are doing so under duress. Sandip in a cold, level voice and cruel determination in his eyes says softly – 'It'll happen here too!' The mask drops completely here and his callous cold-blooded nature is on full display. It is subtle enough to not call undue attention to itself and effective enough to be chilling.

Sandip is a difficult character to play because it does duty both as an individual and as a symbol of a political ideology. Unlike Nikhilesh who (whatever his characterisation in the novel may be) is the very epitome of nobility and goodness and therefore not complex, Sandip is a far more layered creation.

One can compare Sandip to Mayurbahan, even though they are very different characters. They exist in films that cannot be further away from each other, and apart from the presence of Soumitra have nothing in common. Both Sandip and Mayurbahan hide their villainy beneath a façade of suave flamboyance, but while one likes the latter for the colourful rascal that he is, the former is rather repulsive by the end. One may argue that the script and the characters themselves help create this distinction between superficially similar characters, but there is no denying the actor's skill in it. Sandip is a meticulously crafted performance in which Soumitra slowly unfolds the character's true nature.

He says that when it comes to roles where a character slowly reveals his true nature, an actor has to chalk out a kind of action plan. While shooting, it then becomes a matter of execution. There was no problem with the execution. If Sandip has been divisive, it is probably because the film finds it difficult to walk the fine line between narrative and political polemic. The character does not quite lose the awkwardness of being conceived as a character meant to primarily be the spokesperson of an ideology. Soumitra makes him a compelling character, smooth in his villainy, and repugnant in his cowardice.

Proshanto in *Shakha Prosakha* (1990) was the last role Soumitra essayed for Ray. It was not a central character and did not have a lot of screen time. It was however a difficult role because Proshanto was psychologically disturbed, and prone to express his emotions through distinct gestures. Ray, who by this time used to give Soumitra a great deal of freedom, nevertheless gave him very precise directions for this role. He was supposed to bang his hands on the table or on the arm of the sofa in different ways to reflect his response to whatever was going on around him. In *The Master and I* he says that he added a particular mannerism of his own – the regular nodding with which Proshanto kept the measure as he listened to classical music whenever he was disturbed. Soumitra was extremely effective in the role, suggesting his absolute isolation and alienation from everyone around him through an unblinking blank intensity in his eyes. There is also however a keen understanding of the immorality that he sees in his family. In a memorable scene he bangs the table, expressing supreme disgust and pent-up rage.

Ray had given up operating the camera while shooting *Ganashatru*. Soumitra understood that the limitations imposed on him by the doctors were irksome to him in the extreme. Ray had been a workaholic all his life, working tireless twelve-hour days till the wee hours of the morning. Denied external location for shooting, he wrote scripts that were limited in scope and heavy on dialogue. He was alert as ever on the set and as meticulous in his preparations and execution. His last film, *Agantuk*, despite its polemic tone is still a favourite among the Bengali audience. In early 1992, he was ready to shoot his next film with Soumitra in the lead. The script was complete and most of the actors had been cast. It was to go on the floors on 27 February. It was not to be.

Satyajit Ray was hospitalised in January and passed away on 23 April, little more than a week shy of his 71st birthday. Soumitra was shattered. He had lost his father soon after *Charulata*, and this was as terrible a blow to him. He was inconsolable and would later write that the light that had dispelled all darkness in him was gone. Unlike most of the famous director-actor partnerships in the world, there was something distinctly Indian in their mentor-disciple relationship. Soumitra has always said that Ray's contribution to his life went far beyond that of giving him roles in his films. He was part of his life and was part of his family. He went to him with all his questions, and he wrote that Ray was the same to him as his wife and his parents. Ray had discovered him at a young age and had a formative influence on his character. He had learnt a lot about cinema and theatre among other things from him, but what he was most grateful for was something else. Ray had taught him to be an educated, well-rounded artist whose intellectual horizons would perhaps have never been as broad as they were under his paternal stewardship. When he passed away, Soumitra felt rudderless and lost for a long while. In many ways, he still does. He says that he has his memories of him, and that it will be enough to sustain him for the rest of his life. Several decades have passed since his death. Soumitra is an octogenarian now. Nevertheless, when you ask him about Ray, the years slip away, and the cheerful awe of the diligent acolyte takes over easily. He says that he longs to hear his deep baritone voice say 'Soumitra' once more. If that were to happen, he would immediately spring to action again, ready for his shot like he had done once all those years ago as a wide-eyed actor ready to change the world on the sets of *Apur Sansar*.

SIX DECADES IN THE INDUSTRY

STARDOM AND CRITICAL SUCCESS

Soumitra remembers a conversation that he had with Ray during the shooting of *Apur Sansar*. The director was cautioning him about the uncertainties in the life of a professional actor. 'You may not get any other work after this one.' The young Soumitra, with all the heady confidence of youth, knew that there was nothing else he would be happy doing.

He of course got several roles after the success of his first film. As a matter of fact, his first ten years in the industry were remarkably fecund. By 1969, he had already made thirty-eight films, and eighteen of these were made by the leading directors of the time. He had already worked with Ray six times in those ten years. He had also made multiple films with Mrinal Sen, Tapan Sinha, Ajay Kar and Asit Sen.

He was pragmatic enough to understand that while making art house cinema would earn him a lot of critical currency he would have to be part of commercially successful films as well. He had already started working in commercial films in the 1960s but he really began to emerge as a box office star in the 1970s. In this too, he was a little unusual. Most actors first establish their commercial credentials before leveraging that to pursue other more artistically fulfilling endeavours. Uttam Kumar who had to overcome several failures and the humiliating sobriquet 'Flopmaster General' in order to become the biggest draw at the box office did exactly that. Soumitra began his career with a whole slew of art house films that established him as a serious actor before he actively tried to court commercial success.

This may have ensured his eventual success in a way that he could not have anticipated. It was an extremely daunting task to take on Uttam Kumar in the 1960s. Uttam Kumar along with Suchitra Sen had delivered a series of successful films. The characters they played struck a chord with a generation dealing with one of the most traumatic events in recent history. In 1947, Bengal was divided into two along the Radcliffe Line and became West Bengal (part of India) and East Bengal (a province of Pakistan). This Partition led to a mass migration of Bengali Hindus to Calcutta, which soon transformed into a sprawling, chaotic metropolis. The process of this migration was quite often a traumatic and harrowing experience. It left deep psychological scars and unresolved issues of identity, belonging and nostalgia. While Ritwik Ghatak would create the defining cinematic representation of the consequences of Partition in Bengal, commercial cinema would address these issues indirectly and through popular genre forms like melodrama and comedy.

The kind of films that were being made in Bengal after Independence was part of a larger socio-political movement that had its roots in the birth of cinema in India. The studios in Calcutta that were making films for a pan-India audience in the first half of the twentieth century soon lost ground to Bombay which had emerged as the primary centre for film production in Hindi. All through the 1950s, cinema in Bengal gradually moved away from trying to cater to the national audience. In fact, it defined itself in opposition to the Hindi film industry in Bombay. This was a move towards regionalism, and it actively positioned itself as a better class of cinema because it did not believe in the commercial star-based format of Bollywood. The identification of Hindi as a national language during the freedom movement as a means to foster a shared identity was always going to be a problem in a multi-lingual country like India. While Hindi cinema was projected as national cinema, films in any other language were destined to be clubbed under the broad umbrella of regional cinema.

The Bengali film industry was by and large dominated by the middle class until the early 1980s. Consequently, the industry saw itself as better educated, more aesthetically responsible than its counterpart in Bombay for whom cinema was an unabashedly commercial vehicle for the star. In Calcutta, the emphasis was not on the star but on a good story and competent technical standards. This was written about at length in contemporary periodicals (like *Rangalaya* and *Roopmancha*) writing about films in Calcutta. They time and again denounced the exaggerated importance of the star in Bollywood cinema and stuck firmly to their belief in the story as the primary indicator and determinant of a film's worth. This was an important reason why even when Uttam Kumar emerged as the biggest star in the industry, his films would never simply be products cashing in on his widespread appeal.

The breakdown of traditional institutions and communal ties in the aftermath of the Partition and the resulting moral chaos were obliquely addressed through social melodramas. In them the couple have to overcome several obstacles before they can find their happy ending. The centrality of the couple (played by Uttam and Suchitra) in these narratives was important. Their union at the end was a triumph of the individuals and seemed to imply that it could compensate for the losses and confusions faced by the refugees in real life. It was a kind of reorientation in which the individual could now create personal happiness even if historical process had swept away all other certainties of life. Sharmistha Gooptu in her book *Bengali Cinema: An Other Nation* argues that Bengali films in the 1950s was 'emblematic of a generation which had been through the experience of political upheaval and rapid social transition'. It created a new paradigm of what constitutes success and happiness.

Uttam Kumar himself largely broke away from the affected and mannered style of actors like Pramathesh Barua and developed an easy naturalism that mimicked normal idioms and gestures. This was a major step forward, even though it was accomplished within the restricting parameters of commercial cinema. In spite of this attempt at realism in his characters, his larger-than-life aura made Uttam a very big star. His natural confidence made him the quintessential leading man hard coded to play out fantasies of success and self-realisation.

When Ray's *Pather Panchali* came out in 1955, it was a radical shift from the commercial sensibilities of the average melodrama. In *Apur Sansar*, Soumitra played a dreamy, idealistic youth whose search for idyllic happiness is fulfilled for a short while during his marriage with Aparna. The scenes dealing with marital bliss in a realistic yet charming manner was something very new in Bengali cinema. Soumitra says that there were many who came up to him and told him that they would like to get married after watching those scenes. It was fortuitous that Ray had chosen him to play Apu. Soumitra, tall, handsome with sensitive, refined features could very well have been pitted against Uttam Kumar in similar roles. Instead, he was associated with Apu, the thoughtful poetic romantic figure, for whom material concerns were secondary to the life of the spirit. Later when Soumitra carved out a niche for himself in commercial cinema second only to Uttam Kumar, their rivalry would be reduced to a simple binary between a commercial hero and an 'intellectual' hero. This was mostly due to the fact that Soumitra never really strayed from the initial training he had received from Sisir Kumar and Ray. This ensured an important distinction between him and Uttam Kumar. It also led to a very unique career trajectory. Within a decade of *Apur Sansar*, he made a mark at the box office. He would remain a significant box office draw all through the 1970s by finding an extremely effective compromise between his process as an actor and the demands of the box office. He had the good fortune of not only being Ray's 'one-man stock company' but also a big star in commercial cinema. Soumitra has never dismissed his stardom in light of his critically acclaimed roles in more serious films. He is quite proud of the fact that commercial cinema of the 1970s was defined by both Uttam Kumar and Soumitra Chatterjee.

Soumitra had the good fortune of working with Tapan Sinha in only his third film, *Kshudhita Pashan,* in 1960. He remembers learning a lot from the director during its making. Soumitra considered Ray and Tapan Sinha 'actor's directors' because they were actively involved in moulding the performances of the actors in their films. Soumitra who concentrated mostly on psychological naturalism in his early years learnt the techniques of walking in front of the camera and the importance of physicality in performance. He had tried several exercises with weights on his head to get his stepping right. He nevertheless says that it was really Tapan Sinha who taught him to get his gait right. He also showed him how to maintain the position of his shoulders, and instil a rhythm into his movements on camera. It was very important advice for him. He had not really thought too much about it when he was playing Apu, choosing whatever he thought would suit the character best. That probably explains why it may seem slightly rough around the edges at times. He was as usual a good student and in *Jhinder Bondi* (1961), his second film with Tapan Sinha, these lessons led him to turn in a memorable performance as the villain, Mayurbahan.

Tapan Sinha began his career in 1946 in a film production house called New Theatres as a sound engineer. He moved to England in 1950, and for the next two years he made his bones working at the famous Pinewood Studios. Tapan Sinha acknowledged the central influence of British and American filmmakers on his craft. At a time when most filmmakers (including Ray) were inspired by the neo-realists, he stated that it was Jack Conway's 1935 adaptation of Charles Dickens's *A Tale of Two Cities* starring Ronald Colman as Sydney Carton that got him really interested in filmmaking. In a long career spanning several decades he along with Satyajit Ray, Mrinal Sen and Ritwik Ghatak emerged as the greatest filmmakers of their generation.

Tapan Sinha straddled several genres, always at ease in each of them, mostly because he had a gift for narrative storytelling. Nowhere was this more in evidence than in his 1961 adaptation of Saradindu Bandyopadhyay's novel, *Jhinder Bondi*. The novel was largely inspired by Anthony Hope's extremely popular pseudo-historical adventure novel, *The Prisoner of Zenda* (1894). Interestingly enough, Ronald Colman (whom Soumitra adored as well) played the double role of the imprisoned king and the impersonator in the 1937 film version. The role of the dashing yet dangerous villain Rupert of Hentzau was played by Douglas Fairbanks Jr. Rupert was such a popular character that four years after the publication of the novel, Anthony Hope wrote a sequel, *Rupert of Hentzau*, with him as the central character. In Saradindu's version, Rupert's name has been changed to Mayurbahan, the role that Tapan would offer to Soumitra Chatterjee.

Tapan Sinha defended his decision to cast Soumitra, who had only been doing certain kinds of roles for Ray, as the villain by saying that he was sure that he would be able to pull it off. He further pointed out that stars in Hollywood broke away from the mould from time to time, and it was time it was done in Bengal as well. His exposure and direct experience of European cinema made him less rigid about these things, and Soumitra, never particularly wary about taking chances, jumped at the opportunity. If he was apprehensive about anything at all, it was the prospect of working with Uttam Kumar, the biggest star in the industry.

Uttam Kumar, the *Mahanayak*, was a rare phenomenon. An untrained virtuoso, he dominated the industry for nearly three decades in a manner that would perhaps never be surpassed or even replicated. Uttam, handsome and brimming over with charisma, combined a commanding screen presence with an apparently effortless naturalism. He remained the biggest box office draw until his untimely death in 1980 from a heart attack at the age of fifty-three. Soumitra, who came closest in terms of stardom to him, is effusive in his praise for 'Uttam da', his senior by a little more than a decade in the industry. He admits having learnt a lot from him, mostly because despite his superstardom, Uttam also happened to be a naturally gifted performer.

Soumitra, like many others in his generation, would always be a little under the gigantic shadow the *Mahanayak* cast. Soumitra was rather lucky that his career trajectory was to take a very different direction. It helped him to carve out an identity for himself. This also allowed him to stand his own in the long but friendly rivalry that existed between him and Uttam Kumar.

However, when he was given the role of Mayurbahan, Uttam was the reigning superstar for a while. Soumitra who was only twenty-six at the time remembers being rather intimidated at the prospect of working with him. His first scene with him was the one in which Gauri (played by Uttam) tears a medallion off Mayurbahan's neck. Uttam already had the aura of a star that he wore lightly but with confidence. Unhappy at his own performance in the scene, he interrupted it and looked at the director – 'Let's try another take, Tapan da!' This was new for Soumitra, who had never seen anyone but the director cancel the shot. He quickly understood that Uttam was actually taking responsibility for his own performance. He reckons he learnt a valuable lesson that day – an actor is responsible for the shot and he should be able to do it as many times as he wants until he is happy.

Mayurbahan was a challenge for Soumitra. The role of a villain in commercial cinema is no less an artificial creation than a hero. While one is the embodiment of every conceivable virtue, the figure of the villain is generally starkly evil, without any redeeming feature whatsoever. An actor would have to play it with broad strokes, avoiding subtlety and allowing an exaggerated depiction to match the exaggerated characterisation of a stock figure.

Soumitra would never have managed to play it that way. He could not really prepare for it the way he had done with his other roles. With the help of Tapan Sinha, he went about doing something new.

Mayurbahan is arrogant and intelligent with a streak of malevolent humour. During the coronation of the impostor, he shatters the solemnity of the occasion with loud, mocking guffaws. Compared to the worried somberness of the would-be usurper Udit (played by Tarun Kumar), Soumitra's Mayurbahan has flair and panache. The restless energy that was charming in Amal is here injected with an air of menace. He is an equestrian and an expert swordsman. Tapan instructed Soumitra to add a swagger and overbearing confidence to his body language which he did to great effect.

This led to the creation of an extremely interesting villain, multifaceted rather than one-dimensional. In that first scene with Uttam, when the latter snatches the medallion from him, his irreverent conceit gives way to rage and mortification. It is only for an instant though. He regains his supercilious complacency and walks away whistling carelessly. It is an unusual amount of layering for a villain, and in that slight slipping of the mask that reveals his true feelings, Mayurbahan becomes a real person rather than a well played stereotype.

Interestingly enough, the unconventional choice of playing the villainous henchman probably did a lot to increase his popularity among the masses. *Jhinder Bondi* was a major box office success, and the audience could not help but like the wicked, witty and flamboyant Mayurbahan.

Soumitra's decisions as an actor, helped along as they were by excellent teachers, seem well-considered and aimed at creating a new kind of actor star. It was probably fortunate happenstance that even in his first widely popular role (and not just among discerning viewers) he was busy trying to find the truth of the character as Sisir Bhaduri had taught him to do.

In 1965, he worked in Mrinal Sen's *Akash Kusum*. He made two more films in the sixties with Mrinal Sen – *Punascha* and *Pratinidhi*. *Akash Kusum* remains the best of the three. The film attracted a fair bit of negative publicity after it was released. A war of words erupted in the form of newspaper articles between Asish Barman (the film's screenwriter) and Satyajit Ray who found the protagonist's motivations logically untenable. However, Sen's use of New Wave cinema techniques like freeze frames and jump cuts meant that it was less a neo-realist film and more a forerunner of the *Nouvelle Vague* in India.

As a fable, the story works fine, and Soumitra as Ajay plays an unscrupulous and ambitious urban young man with easy confidence. There are similarities with the protagonist of Theodore Dreiser's *An American Tragedy* (a film version called *A Place in the Sun* starring Montgomery Clift in one of his greatest roles was released in 1951). Ajay's desperate trickery reflected the reorientation of youthful ambition towards definite materialistic goals. Ajay, like many of the protagonists of the films of that decade, embodied the confusion and frustration consequent upon a conflict between an older and ancient set of codes and beliefs and modern attitudes that were at the other end of the spectrum. In his fervent enthusiasm along with the impracticality of his ruse to win over Manika (played by Aparna Sen) he is the urban counterpart of Apu. Yet, he has none of his artistic idealism, and his ambitions are nakedly materialistic. At the end of the film, his dishonesty is discovered, and as Manika waves him a tearful farewell, it is not just deserved punishment for fraudulent behaviour. It is the just consequence of the inherent confusion of values that prompted him to act in that way to begin with. Soumitra translates the unscrupulousness of Mayurbahan into a far more realistic mould, significantly increasing the depth of the character by adding subtle layers like a painter achieving depth through judicious layering of his colours.

He is by turns, arrogant, insecure, shy and boisterous, building his character from the ground up, and adding verisimilitude to a story that operates more like a fable than otherwise. He ties the plot firmly to the ground, instinctively instilling realism in a character to which everyone of that generation could easily relate.

Baksa Badal, which came out in 1970, was directed by Nityananda Datta, Soumitra's very good friend. It was Netai (when he was working as part of Satyajit Ray's crew) who had insisted that he should go and meet Satyajit Ray for *Aparajito*. The shadow of his former boss looms large over the film, not least because the script was written by Ray himself. There were at the time unkind rumours that Ray had ghost directed the entire film and allowed his former assistant to take the credit. Soumitra dismisses these rumours outright. He does not deny that Ray spent a lot of time in the studio while it was being made. However, he definitely was not around for the long schedule in Kalimpong.

Ray had enough confidence in Netai to carry it off.

Ray's script was adapted from a short story by Bibhutibhushan Bandyopadhyay, a delightful comedy full of misunderstandings, disguises and a happy resolution. It was a breezy, light-hearted affair that gave Soumitra an opportunity to try out his comic chops. Eventually comedy would become Soumitra's favourite genre, because it gave him a chance to take a break from more demanding roles and kick back and have fun.

Soumitra admired the literary foundation of the script. He always looked forward to acting in films that were adapted from novels, short stories and plays. He reckons that a director or scriptwriter would do well to read as much as possible. He was also excited because Ray had written the script. He felt that the role of a psychiatrist was something no one had done before in Bengali cinema.

Ray's script follows a simple three-act structure. It uses all the contrivances of comedy like mistaken identity, deception and intrigue to keep the plot tight and interesting. Nityananda's sure-footed direction, location shooting at the picturesque Kalimpong, and snappy editing by Ramesh Joshi ensured that

Soumitra with film director Mrinal Sen
Photo courtesy of Pratap Dasgupta

Baksa Badal was a big hit. The snappy chemistry between Soumitra and Aparna, with whom he would star in several successful films, also established them as a commercially viable pairing.

Soumitra plays Pratul Bhattacharya, a psychiatrist who has to later disguise himself as Pramod Bhattacharya. Pramod is not really supposed to be different from Pratul, especially because it has been done for the benefit of Amita (played by Aparna Sen) who has never met Pratul before. It would have been rather strange if Soumitra had played Pramod as a completely different person when it was not required.

He very cleverly used make-up, wardrobe and even something as simple as combing his hair a different way to create a striking visual difference between the two characters. He also subtly changes his behaviour as Pramod. He is less cocksure, more pleasant and friendly. Even more importantly, he proved that when it came to comic timing, he could go toe to toe with the best of them. If it was difficult to compete with Uttam Kumar at the box office, it was equally difficult to be accepted as a comic actor.

Ever since the release of Dhiren Ganguly's *Bilet Pherat* in 1921, comedy was one of the most commonly produced genres in Bengali cinema. When Soumitra was starting his career, the Bengali film industry was flush with comic talents of the highest order. Soumitra had thoroughly enjoyed both *Saare Chuattor* (1953) and *Ora Thaake Odhaare* (1954), Uttam Kumar-Suchitra Sen starrers populated by the most popular comic actors of the time like Tulsi Chakrobarty, Bhanu Bandyopadhyay, Jahar Ray, Nabadweep Haldar, Shyam Laha among others. Tulsi Chakraborty in particular was a self-taught genius who had no formal training in acting and had in fact started his career as a clown in the circus in Burma (Myanmar). He brought an unvarnished down-to-earth reality to his roles which informed by his superlative comic timing made him one of the greatest comic actors of any era. Ray who had cast him as the protagonist of his *Parash Pathar* (1958) was in awe of his tremendous natural talent. He would later recount how Tulsi Chakraborty was among the very few to whom he never had to give any acting notes.

Soumitra was therefore working in a well-established genre when he took up the role of Pratul Bhattacharya in *Baksa Badal*. It is not surprising that he brought his usual cerebral approach to the role. The plot itself is about a romantic relationship which once initiated must run the course of the usual hurdles and distractions before it can reach its happy resolution. The end is a foregone conclusion, and the audience's interest depends on the telling of it. Nityananda told it well, and Soumitra and Aparna Sen helped along by a strong cast did the rest.

At the beginning of the film, when Pratul realises that the box belongs to someone else, he starts going through its contents. He pauses after a while, and gingerly brings out a piece of woman's underwear. He scrutinises it with ill-concealed bewilderment. He then suddenly drops it, snaps back stiffly and firmly says 'Impossible!' The whole thing is done smoothly, with his slow dismay at finding the bit of clothing contrasting neatly with his sudden, sharp one-word dismissal.

Soumitra while speaking of the difficult art of making people laugh makes a distinction between two kinds of comedy. One way to do it would be to use physical laughter or funny dialogue, like in a Buster Keaton or a Marx brothers film. In the other way the humour would lie in the treatment of the material. The actors and situations are normal enough, but the plotting and angle of narration make them comic. He considered the latter approach a more sophisticated one.

Soumitra knew the value of a well-delivered line in comedy, and he drew on his own experiences of talking to people whom he knew were funny in real life. He also carefully identified humorous lines in the script and was very particular about delivering them with the right intonation and timing.

In 1969 he starred in Ashutosh Bandyopadhyay's *Teen Bhubaner Paare* with Tanuja. The story was based on a short story by Samaresh Basu. Soumitra who knew Samaresh Basu, met him before starting work on the film. The author told him that he had based the character on a real person, and he even pointed this person out to him. The film was supposed to be a mainstream picture but Soumitra was happy to know that he would be playing someone based on a real person.

Soumitra plays Subir, a young factory hand who has to support his family. He spends most of his idle hours wandering around with his unemployed friends. Hemmed in by poverty and lack of opportunities, they act out in ways that scandalise the conservative members of the community for whom they are nothing but troublemakers. Subir was the quintessential 'loafer', a pejorative term that had come into popular usage during that milieu. It usually referred to individuals who would hang around at street corners all day and harass passersby. There was more to this though. Subir not only has to bear the financial burden for his entire family but also has to deal with a deadening and exhausting job at the factory and a cantankerous father at home.

His pent-up frustrations naturally find expression in acts of recklessness and obstreperous behaviour. Soumitra brings the requisite level of sincerity and depth to the character, raising him from just a rowdy 'loafer' to a complex character with whom the audience could sympathise and even relate. A simple trope of redemption through love became an ideal vehicle for the kind of star that Soumitra was destined to become. He was adept at finding strains of authenticity even in characters that were meant for commercial cinema. With a keen eye on the truth of a role, Soumitra could not but help individualise every character he played. This has been largely responsible for the distinctive position he holds in the annals of Bengali and, indeed, Indian film history.

While it may be some curious combination of accident and deliberate thought that was responsible for this, it certainly was not easy. A conventional leading man in commercial cinema had to be adept at a number of things that may or may not have anything strictly to do with acting. This included being able to fight convincingly and dancing, both of which were considered necessary parts of a leading man's skill set. If an actor was associated with a hit song, his popularity would be significantly boosted. Yet, there were no designated experts in the industry back then. Later there would be choreographers and directors for both fights and dancing but Soumitra did not have anyone to really show him the ropes.

In *Teen Bhubaner Paare*, he had to dance to the extremely popular '*Jibone ki pabona'* as part of a group of local folks celebrating a win in a football match in the very first sequence of the film. Later in the film, he would woo Sarasi (Tanuja) as she is returning from work with another huge hit '*Ke tumi Nandini*'. Both these songs were composed and written by Sudhin Dasgupta and sung by Manna Dey.

Soumitra was not exactly unprepared though. He had already spent some time learning ballroom dancing from the veteran trainer Bob Das. Nevertheless, dancing in film was a different animal altogether. He was not blind to its importance in commercial cinema. He admits that Uttam Kumar was a much better dancer than he could ever be. The superstar had undergone a lot of training, while Soumitra had to approach it the only way he could – by trying to infuse a touch of realism in it. His performance as a dancer in '*Jibone ki pabona*' is a little stilted and awkward, which in a strange way becomes a more authentic representation of how someone who's just come on the road to celebrate a sports victory would dance. Even his pursuit of the heroine in '*Ke tumi Nandini*' is filmed in a way that is a little less artificial and staged than the manner in which a song starring Uttam and Suchitra would be presented. And since the latter pair was the gold standard as far as commercial Bengali cinema was concerned, the only way was to better Uttam at his own game or do something different. Soumitra chose to go the other way.

The songs of *Teen Bhubaner Paare* eventually gained a kind of popularity that quite surpassed the film itself. They became the staple of almost all functions, gatherings and can sometimes be heard even today blaring out of loudspeakers during the many pujas that dot the religious calendar of Bengal. A popular song's repeatability in an age where there was no way of watching a film after its theatrical run was over ensured the continuing popularity of the actor associated with it. *Teen Bhubaner Paare* which was a very big hit at the box office along with *Basanta Bilap* cemented his status as a bankable star second only to Uttam Kumar.

Soumitra has played comic roles with both subtle variations and broad differences. His innate flexibility allowed him to approach each of these roles according to the conventions of the genre. The subtle comicality of Amulya in *Samapti* would be quite out of place in a film that depended on broad humour. *Basanta Bilap* which was released in 1973 was Soumitra's fiftieth film. This was a fair indication of how busy he had been in the last fourteen years. *Basanta Bilap* which was yet another major commercial success for Soumitra was directed by Dinen Gupta. Dinen was an extremely talented cinematographer who had shot two masterpieces by Ritwik Ghatak, *Ajantrik* and *Meghe Dhaka Tara*. He had however chosen a straightforward comedy with a screenplay written by Shekhar Chatterjee for his directorial venture.

By this time in his career, Soumitra had gained enough confidence to not be intimidated by the presence of Anup Kumar, Robi Ghosh and Chinmoy Roy, three of the biggest comic actors of the time. He fancied his chances even though he would generally always be seen with them. The plot of the film is a series of loosely connected incidents designed to elicit laughter through horseplay and dialogue. In comedic terms, Soumitra's role as Shyam is more of a straight man whose sole purpose in the film is to take revenge for all the times he has been insulted by Anuradha (played by Aparna Sen). He is assisted by his posse of troublemakers who carry the primary comedic burden of the story.

Soumitra thought he would succeed in entertaining the audience but he was also the first to admit that it was not an easy task. It did not take him very long to figure out that comedy would require a different approach as an actor. He says that it is important for an actor to recognise the humour in a scene. He has to really feel it because unless the actor finds it funny, he will never be able to make the audience laugh. He recalls that he found the interactions with Anuradha in which they trade insults in their respective offices inherently funny, and once he saw that he knew what the audience would find funny as well.

This did not mean that he left the broader bits to his co-stars. At the end of the film, he infiltrates the women's hostel disguised as an old man. His antics, exaggerated and hammy, play straight to the gallery. He had to dance here too. In the absence of a choreographer, it was up to him to come up with steps that were funny without going unacceptably over the top. It worked too, and its no small feat that even when it came to roles in mainstream cinema, he was careful enough to make sure that they do not seem like the same person. It says a fair bit about him as an artist that he was able to calibrate his performances on screen to reflect the requirements of the genre. The fact that he was successful is amply displayed by how successful the film was at the box office. Like *Teen Bhubaner Paare*, this too has a couple of hit songs, '*Aami Miss Calcutta*' and '*Aagun*'. Manna Dey who had sung '*Aagun*' was particularly fond of Soumitra's performance in it. He had listened to the song multiple times until he knew it inside out. It also imparted a relaxed flow to his performance. This kind of preparation was responsible for the easy charm he exuded in these films.

The success of these films was also due to the laid-back and fun times the actors had while shooting them. Dinen Gupta later said that things were always slightly riotous with three comic actors of that calibre on set. Their antics also entertained everyone around them. He recalled how he had wanted to take a shot of Soumitra facing Anup Kumar, the latter's back to the camera. He had implored Anup Kumar to not make faces at Soumitra because he would never be able to give the shot properly. Anup was incorrigible, and Soumitra would crack up every time. Dinen ruefully said that he had to change the entire shot. While shooting a holi sequence, Anup jumped up into Soumitra's arms and stayed there. Dinen, who had to interrupt the shot, hauled him up and asked him to explain himself. Anup, with the straightest face possible, stated that he was only following his director's instruction asking him to put some *aabir* on Soumitra's face. He pointed out that since Soumitra was fairly tall he could not think of any other way of accomplishing that. That had the entire crew in splits. Their high-spirited camaraderie on the sets translated well into their fellowship on screen.

Teen Bhubaner Paare and *Basanta Bilap* played a significant role in moulding Soumitra's legacy in the public imagination. Long before globalisation and cable changed the landscape of television in India and Bengal, there was just the state-run Doordarshan that from the 1970s onwards would show reruns of Bengali films. For those who grew up in those times, the sole Bengali film that would be broadcast on Sunday evenings was something to really look forward to. These two films were pretty standard fare for these Sunday evening broadcasts. Repeated telecasts ensured that as far as commercial films were concerned, these are the roles with which he became primarily associated in the public imagination.

In the 1970s, Soumitra was a bonafide star. He never tried to directly compete with Uttam Kumar, which in the circumstances was probably the wise thing to do. His unusual trajectory which led from critically acclaimed roles to stardom instead of the other way around was also responsible for determining the kind of star he would be. Soumitra tried his hand at all the popular genres of the time – thrillers, comedies, romantic films, and drama. He was led by his natural tendencies as well as by his training to find (even at the most superficial level possible) and portray the authenticity of whichever character came his way.

Soumitra has said in multiple interviews that he never wanted his stardom to come between him and potentially good roles. This meant a deliberate refusal to cultivate a well-liked persona carefully built and maintained to appeal to the widest cross-section of the audience. It was perhaps a little easier for him than it would have been for any other person in his position. His penchant for finding the individuality in a role that would connect it to the reality of people in the actual world worked counter to creating a self-replicating persona on screen. Consequently, the audience never saw him as a larger-than-life superstar like Uttam Kumar whose on-screen persona had an aura that removed it from mundane reality. Soumitra was always one of them, a person they think they might actually have seen and known in real life. This sympathetic credibility and the sincerity of his performances gained him immense popularity in the first two decades of his career. This also meant that he had carved a very unique niche for himself. He was, without belabouring the point too much, a star because he was a very good actor. This is rare enough to never have been replicated again in Bengali cinema.

1980S ONWARDS – A PARADIGM SHIFT

Bengali cinema went through a serious paradigmatic shift in the late 1970s due to a number of reasons. From the 1950s, the middle class that had dominated the industry represented Bengali cinema as superior to what was being produced in Bombay. Bengali cinema has traditionally been hostile to the notion that it is regional cinema and therefore insular and somehow less important because of that. It is therefore a little ironic that when the shift in the industry occurred in the 1980s, it survived by the skin of its teeth only by copying the conventions of Hindi commercial cinema.

Several factors were changing the orientation of Bengali cinema in the late 1970s. There were a number of disputes between the producers and exhibitors-distributors that effectively led the latter to shift loyalties to Hindi films. Bombay paid better, and the common grievance in the 1980s was that many Bengali films did not see the light of day because the exhibitors were not interested. The Hindi film industry offered a slick, technically superior product and strengthened their market presence in Bengal. Meanwhile, the urban middle class that was the mainstay of the industry and among its primary consumers was gradually moving away from cinema to television. Uttam Kumar's untimely death in 1980 effectively marked the end of a whole era and modus operandi of filmmaking. For better or for worse, with everything changing, the industry was in crisis and on the cusp of a comprehensive transformation.

The kind of films that saved the industry shifted its focus away from Calcutta to the suburbs and villages. They chose characters from less-advantaged classes as their protagonists and preached sermons of social justice in broad melodramatic tones. The harbinger of this change, and in many ways the seminal film of this new era, was Anjan Choudhury's *Shatru*, which was released in 1984. The storytelling was unashamedly borrowed from Hindi potboilers. It made fight sequences, song-and-dance routines and the other accessories of commercial Bollywood cinema part of the new imitative lexicon of Bengali popular cinema. The target audience was now the poorer classes from villages and small towns. Films like *Beder Meye Jyotsna* were widely panned for their theatrical performances and unsophisticated filmmaking, but they made enough money to keep the industry afloat till a new generation of filmmakers could pick up the aesthetic slack. Soumitra was now middle-aged and belonged in every way to a generation that had all but disappeared. (Ray's films in the 1980s were almost like hothouse flowers that were thoroughly disconnected from the general mainstream tendencies in the industry.) Therefore he was facing a crisis as well.

Later he said that there were several moments in his career when he thought that the audience would desert him. He would then have no choice but to pack up and leave, trusting his reputation to the kindness of history. He may have had such thoughts in these transitional years. Yet, the same instinct for survival and flexibility that had guided him unerringly through the first two decades of his career, ensured that he emerged from this largely unscathed. He was the greatest living actor in Bengal, and while he may not have wanted to do some of the films he had to do, he tried to do them with all the professionalism at his disposal. In this too, he was thankful to his mentor. He recalled how Ray had seen him in his younger days betray a hint of contempt while acting in a film. He

> One of the lesser known facts about Soumitra is that apart from working in Bengali films, he has acted in two Hindi films (*Nirupama* and *Hindustani Sipahi*), as well as in an Anglo-French production, *The Bengali Night* (French: *La Nuit Bengali*) released in 1988.
>
> The film, shot almost entirely in Kolkata, was based on a semi-autobiographical Romanian novel by Mircea Eliade and directed by Nicolas Klotz. *The Bengali Night* also starred Hugh Grant, Shabana Azmi and Supriya Pathak. Soumitra's fluency and effortless proficiency in the English language stands out as does his stunning looks.

was used to working with Ray by then, and being a young man had not quite been able to hide his disdain while working with someone less talented than the master. Ray was annoyed with him, and ticked him off for being unprofessional. He told him that if he had taken on the role and was being paid for it, it was his duty, irrespective of every other consideration, to give his best in front of the camera. He took this lesson to heart and maintained a level of professionalism that was responsible for the longevity of his career in spite of the great changes in the industry since the time he had started out.

In the third decade of his career he had to take on different roles because of his advancing age, and also slowly evolve his craft to suit the changing circumstances. It is not surprising that he managed to do both fairly successfully.

Among the films that he did during this phase, he remembers *Agradani* with great fondness. It released in 1983 and was inspired by a novel by Tarashankar Bandyopadhyay. Soumitra had already acted in Ray's adaptation of Tarashankar's *Abhijaan*. *Agradani* was however a very different film. Soumitra was quite keen to take on the role because he had read the novel during his college days. He looked forward to the challenge of portraying the life of a man from his youth to his old age. It would also call upon him to explore a wide range of techniques, some of which were removed from the muted realism that he had employed for the majority of his career.

Photo courtesy of Supriyo Nag

Soumitra has always defended this film even though it is sloppily made and depends too much on melodrama all through. He thinks that it has a strong narrative. Besides, this is the role that made him popular in the suburbs and villages. The unabashed sentimentality of the narrative and the well-timed broad emotional beats made it immensely popular. However in terms of the absence of subtlety and thematic depth, it was symptomatic of the creative decline that the industry was going through because of its radical reorientation. The material itself could have been translated well by more competent filmmakers. As such, the inherent poignancy of the story still manages to make it a moving cinematic experience.

The real challenge that Soumitra perhaps faced was to somehow attune his naturally realistic method to the heightened melodramatic tone of the film itself. The role of Purna Chakraborty was rooted in an ancient tradition. The *agradani* was a Brahmin whose primary function was to be part of funerals where he would be a stand-in for the departed and receive gifts from his relatives. In spite of this seemingly important position, the *agradani* Brahmin was at the lower end of the strict hierarchical structure within the Brahmin community. Tarashankar's novel ends with the protagonist being forced to act as the *agradani* at his own son's funeral. It is a devastating ending and one can see that in Soumitra's desolate face at the end of the film.

It had been ten years since his masterful portrayal of a village Brahmin in Ray's *Ashani Sanket*. He brought to Purna Chakraborty some of the mannerisms

On the sets, with make-up, for one of his latter day films
Photo courtesy of Supriyo Nag

and body language that he had learnt during his extensive research for Gangacharan a decade ago. Nonetheless this is where the similarities ended. There is a degree of broad humour at the beginning. We are introduced to Purna enacting the role of Hanuman in a *jatra*. This exaggerated style of acting is in a large measure carried over to the rest of the performance as well.

Soumitra understood the importance of retaining the authenticity of the emotions he is portraying although the gestures, facial expressions and even dialogue delivery would be heightened and exaggerated. He straddles this fine line well. Consequently he ensures that the flaws in the filmmaking are compensated for by his moving portrayal. This was something new as far as he was concerned. He had made several commercial films before in his career but the tone and craft of commercial cinema was different then. He did not really have to modulate his entire approach drastically in order to work in them. And so, even if there were lapses in narrative or deficiencies in the script, the general aesthetic approach was standardised enough to not clash too much with his style of acting.

In a film like *Agradani*, the plot is strung together by his performance alone, which in turn meant that there was greater responsibility on him. The popularity that the character gained means that he had fundamentally succeeded in this. He however did not abandon realism and give himself over to *jatra* in order to achieve that. There is exaggeration in his performance, to be sure. A purist used to seeing him act in the films of Ray, Mrinal Sen, and Tapan Sinha would be tempted to dismiss this kind of performance as one playing to the gallery. Yet, there is significant craft involved here too.

Later in the film, Purna goes to visit his son who is studying in Calcutta. His son is visibly ashamed of his rustic father and, in a scene rife with manipulative sentimentality, he introduces him to his obnoxious and rude friend as 'an old servant'. Purna of course thinks that an old servant is English for father. He comes back home rather proud of his son's command over the English language. There follows an extended sequence in which he goes about telling everyone about this new phrase he has learned from his son. Inevitably, he finds out the truth and is deeply hurt. This extended sequence designed to elicit compassion and pity for the protagonist is blatantly mawkish. Soumitra nevertheless concedes very little to the general tenor of the scenes, bringing genuine pride to his manner as he goes about the village, and then real sadness at the discovery.

This near continuous strain of authenticity in an otherwise amplified performance made the film watchable and accounted for its popularity. It would also be the cornerstone of his approach to films in a decade of significant adjustment and change. He regulated his techniques to suit the shifting attitudes to filmmaking, ensuring his continuing relevance in the industry. It also meant that as he transitioned into roles meant for middle-aged and eventually elderly actors, he would always be sought after simply by virtue of the fact that even though tastes were changing, he was still the go-to person for roles that required serious skill.

Sensible though they were, these adjustments, notwithstanding his professionalism, were not something he had enjoyed making. He had decided to take up acting as a vocation for very specific reasons. His favourite actor on screen was Balraj Sahni, an educated man who was associated with the advent of realist cinema in Bollywood. His mentor in theatre and acting in general was Sisir Kumar Bhaduri, the leading actor of his generation. His foray into films was engineered by Satyajit Ray. Compared to so many others who have tried their luck in this fickle industry, Soumitra was unusually lucky that he was the right man at the right place. It also meant that he had rather high expectations from himself and from films in general.

This was why he grew steadily more and more disillusioned with the quality of films produced in Bengal after the 1980s. In his writings, he is bitter about the many compromises he has had to make simply because he had to earn his living. One cannot keep on indefinitely waiting for good films, he says. He has had to make films that were subpar from every possible point of view.

He says that working in those films left him dejected, depressed and extremely fatigued. He had started on a high note of hope, and he was sure that he had begun his career during the dawn of a new age in Bengali cinema. Yet it turned out to be temporary and ended all too soon. Once he had to take

Soumitra in a contemplative mood
Photo courtesy of Supriyo Nag

on roles that he did not want, it became a chore and he has admitted to feeling rather helpless at the state of things.

He definitely does not like that he has to do them because he has to think of money over any other consideration. He has always been high-minded about acting and the real function of films. He admits that he had wanted fame and popularity in his youth. He had started out when Uttam Kumar had already become a star. As a young man he wanted a share of the immense popularity the superstar enjoyed. He says that this desire waned eventually.

Soumitra with actor Mithun Chakraborty
Photo courtesy of Supriyo Nag

Besides, it was always subservient to his overriding ambition to do good roles. Unfortunately, an actor must also contend with the inherent uncertainty of his profession, and it can compel one to put a higher premium on the next available paycheck or the safe popular choice more often than not. Soumitra's career has to be defined in terms of him having had the upper hand in this conflict.

His appetite for good roles and his ambition as an actor have overwhelmed all other questions. He has spent the better part of his life honing and perfecting his craft. It has not been easy, he says, and has required a good deal of dedication and hard work. He has had to make sacrifices too in order to stay true to this ambition as an artist. When film aesthetics in Bengal took a decided turn for the worse, he felt that all this hard work would now be wasted. He is quite candid about the fact that he has flouted his own principles and taken roles he did not want. It is perhaps a helpful defence mechanism. If he can admit where he has compromised, it leaves the legacy of his serious performances intact. One would not then necessarily taint the other.

The lack of intellectuality in contemporary commercial cinema bothers him, especially because his love for cinema and his intellectual flowering during his youth in Calcutta (and subsequent experiences with Sisir Kumar and Ray) are inseparable in his memory. What was worse was perhaps the feeling that he is not being challenged in any way, and that his experience and craft would eventually rust with disuse. Soumitra has written at length about acting in cinema, and he fondly remembers the little things that would inspire him to go over and beyond for certain directors. When he was filming *Ashani Sanket*, there was a scene being shot late in the evening where he had to go to someone's house to ask for some rice. He recalls that at that point, the famine was in full spate, and Gangacharan is both famished and thirsty. A bit of desperation has crept into his body language. He chose to accentuate this nervous despair with a slight gulp. It was a subtle gesture, and Ray who was usually monosyllabic after he okayed a shot said 'Excellent!' It was a moment of great pride for him. In the later years of his career, the memories of working with the great directors of the past would cause significant distress to him. He says he has managed to keep going because he has not allowed this cynicism to turn into despair. He would not be able to do anything then. He has countered this bitterness with a constant enthusiasm for whatever new project is close to his heart. In his later years, these projects have had more to do with his work in the theatre than in films.

This is not to say that he has not acted in good films during this period. His criticism has been directed more at the general than at the particular. In fact, he counts several performances from this time among his favourites. Quite possibly, the best among these and the closest to his heart is Khitish Sinha or Khit da from *Kony* (1984). In several interviews he has admitted that whenever he faces personal troubles or physical and psychological ailments, he keeps repeating the famous dialogue from *Kony* to himself, 'Fight, Kony, fight.' In his long career where he has worked with almost all the greats of his time, he considers *Kony* to be among the very best he has made.

Kony was a special film for him. Soumitra has been a lifelong sports enthusiast. As a boy growing up in Krishnanagar, he spent a lot of time outdoors playing and running around. There was also his uncle, who was a skilled sportsman and whom he admired a lot. He would bring back trophies and medals that he would stare at with awe. It instilled in him a love for sports at a very young age. He remembers how in his school days, especially when he was a student at Howrah Zillah School, he would participate in every possible sports the school had to offer. His enthusiasm for sports continued well into his college days. He ruefully recalls how he could not make it to his college cricket team. They were the reigning champions and he admits that he really was not a good enough batsman. He fared better as a hockey player and even played on the Maidan in the second division league for 'Town Club'. He was in Calcutta by then, and his interests increased manifold and threatened to pull him in all kinds of directions at once. His passion for sports struggled with his interest in literature, cinema and theatre. An intellectually curious youth can find new interests that consume him at every turn. Around that time, Gourmohan Mukhopadhyay, his senior in college, cautioned him and told him that he needed greater focus. Soumitra understood the wisdom of these words, and reluctantly withdrew from active participation in sports. His love for sports survived unabated, and even

Soumitra in an outdoor shoot
Photo courtesy of Supriyo Nag

Soumitra on the sets with actor Debashree Roy
Photo courtesy of Supriyo Nag

Soumitra with actor Aparna Sen
Photo courtesy of Supriyo Nag

contributed to his chosen vocation. He believes that the greatest legacy of his love for sports has been his obsession with physical fitness. He was driven to keep himself in good physical condition. This was necessary not just for looking trim and well in his roles, but also for enduring long, punishing schedules that would have completely exhausted a less fit person.

He recounts meeting his favourite sportsmen, especially cricketers, with unabashed glee. He adores Sachin Tendulkar and Sourav Ganguly, but one of his favourite anecdotes is about meeting Sunil Gavaskar. He was standing in queue to board a flight for London when he discovered Gavaskar standing right behind him. He told him that he was a great fan of his batting and he was glad that he finally had the opportunity to tell him that. When he tried to introduce himself Gavaskar interrupted him and smilingly said, 'Mr Soumitra Chatterjee, of course!'

When he got the chance to play Khitish Sinha (Khit da) in *Kony*, he was overjoyed. The film was directed by Saroj Dey who adapted it from a novella by Moti Nandi. The film won awards and, more importantly, became one of those landmarks in popular culture that ensures the continuing popularity of a film for a very long time.

Soumitra had read the novella when it had come out as part of Puja publications, and he was immediately attracted to the character of Khitish Sinha. However, a few years were to pass before the role came to him. He was still doing films as the leading man, and this was yet another opportunity to go into uncharted territory. He did some research into the technicalities of competitive swimming. He did not however immerse himself into the technical details to the extent that he had for other roles. He says that he learnt as much was necessary to play the role. He believed that it was far more essential to pour his enduring love for sports into the character. There was indeed such a measure of his own personality in it, that the authenticity of the performance alone struck a chord with the audience. If Khit da is one of the most beloved characters he has played, it is because he is playing a version of his own self. The sincerity creates a strong emotional connection.

Soumitra went about creating the character from the ground up. He visited a number of swimming clubs in north and central Calcutta, and closely observed how they went about their job. He created the entire look for Khit da based on his observations. His close-cropped hair, dark tan and thick glasses changed his look ridding it of the trappings associated with his star persona. He also gave it individual touches – half-sleeved kurtas, a particular way of wearing the dhoti, and the watch on the inside of the wrist so that he would have to turn his wrist to look at the time. The director not surprisingly had no problem with any of this.

It was not his passion for sports that alone informed his excitement to play the role. Khit da embodied a philosophy of sports that disdained money and fame as secondary to the true objective of a sportsperson. Even more importantly, he was wholly dedicated to supporting and encouraging those who did not have much money. His incorruptible egalitarianism was as much a distillation of his political ideals as it was about his love for sports.

Khit da has remained an inspiring figure. His dedication to his principles, refusal to bow down in adversity, disdain of mean and petty wranglings make him a middle-class ideal. The appeal of Khit da was largely emotional and spoke to the half-articulated aspirations and beliefs of Bengali society in the early 1980s. Therefore its merit cannot be judged on the basis of Soumitra's skills as an actor. He instinctively understood that the only way to sell this character was to play it with all the sincerity at his disposal. A character that embodies all heart and a stubborn desire to overcome all odds has to be understood in the context of whether the actor has successfully captured these qualities. Soumitra's inherent love for the subject made sure of that, and Khit da became an integral part of Bengali pop culture in a way comparable to his other great role, that of Feluda.

Soumitra continued to churn out powerful performances all through the last decades of the twentieth century. Ray had wanted to adapt Buddhadev Basu's *Ekti Jiban* but it never worked out. When Raja Mitra finally made the film it was plagued by financial constraints and took the better part of six years to complete. It released to critical acclaim in 1990 and Soumitra's performance in it received widespread praise. He followed this up with *Wheelchair* in 1995, his last film with Tapan Sinha, in which he plays a paraplegic doctor. The performance is one of his finest hours on screen and was indeed so convincing that a paraplegic on a wheelchair came to thank him after watching the film for conveying what he felt due to his disability. In all these roles, his willingness to go the extra mile to bring a modicum of authenticity to the characters made each of them stand out.

These roles that were now tending towards middle-aged characters took their cue from the inspirational and popular Khit da from *Kony*. So it is no surprise that all of them were about slightly larger-than-life people who embody a noble and upright idealism. The general image of Soumitra Chatterjee in the sphere of popular culture began to shift from that of a romantic lead in commercial movies and versatile actor in more serious cinema. He was by now the leading actor in Bengal, an elder statesman of cinema associated with the golden age of Bengali cinema. The noble aura of the characters he was now playing was seeping into the general conception of him as a person. In time, this would ossify into a kind of veneration that would transform Soumitra into an iconic figure, a multifaceted symbol of different aspects of Bengali high culture.

Soumitra with actor Prosenjit Chatterjee
Photo courtesy of Prosenjit Chatterjee

In 1986, he played the role of a schoolteacher in Tapan Sinha's *Atanka*, a role that endured in the public imagination as much as that of Khit da in *Kony*. Known only as 'Sir' in the film, the protagonist represents an educated, civilised and enlightened class, a not unlikely future manifestation of the iconic Apu. He inadvertently witnesses a murder and his life becomes a miserable, nightmarish medley of intimidation, assault and fear. Sir is no hero and he is distressed and scared. Eventually he finds the courage to stand up against his tormentors and triumphs against them. Here again, Soumitra uses make-up and costume very effectively to downplay his usual charismatic persona and subtly inhabit the skin of a timid, cultured teacher whose life has been turned upside down. *Atanka* was directed by Tapan Sinha. He deeply regretted not having worked with Soumitra for all the years since his first films with the actor in the sixties. He was bowled over by his performance and later said that it

Undeterred by the pandemic Soumitra continues shooting. Still from the shoot of *Abhijaan* directed by Parambrata Chattopadhyay and produced by Ratan Shree Nirman and Roadshow Films Pvt. Ltd.
Photo courtesy of Parambrata Chattopadhyay

required a deep sensitivity and experience to have played this role. It was about a timid man finding his courage. For the most part though 'Sir' is hounded by fear and paranoia, and an anguished distress is the keynote of the character. Soumitra has written a lot about acting and he makes important points about realistic acting. He points out that realistic acting in point of technical fact has nothing to do with realism at all. It is a very deliberately contrived performance that approximates acceptable representation of realistic behaviour on screen. If an actor mimics how we actually behave in real life then ironically enough it will seem exaggerated and unnatural. Soumitra says that acting in cinema is mostly 'underacting', where one dials down one's facial expressions for it to look effectively real. It calls attention to a truism in all art that realism can only be achieved through a mastery of a very manufactured craft. In a film like *Atanka* that required him to depict extreme fear and distress, Soumitra's histrionic skill that is both subtle and controlled pitches these primary responses just right. When it is time for him to assert himself, he keeps the transition understated, thereby making it all the more convincing. It is as much an indication of a master in full control of his craft than anything else.

In the eighth decade of his life, Soumitra continues to work. He has naturally enough slowed down, and grateful directors are more than happy to accommodate the limited hours he can spare on a daily basis for their projects. The roles he now gets are generally the same, that of the ageing patriarch, and it would not be too wrong to say that in most cases, he can do them in his sleep. In 2015, he acted in *Belaseshe*, directed by Nandita Roy and Shiboprosad Mukherjee, for which he received critical appreciation. He played the patriarch of an extended family who decides to divorce his wife of many decades and the film deals with the fallout of the decision. Swatilekha Sengupta, with whom he was working with for the first time since *Ghare-Baire*, played his wife. As an extended meditation on the pitfalls and complexities of marital relationships across several generations, the film does not demand much from Soumitra who plays the role with easy authority. However, as an actor his function has probably transcended the need to find new and unexpected challenges. He brings a hefty seriousness and prestige to all his projects. Most directors are happy to leverage the artistic currency that his presence brings to claim artistic seriousness for their films. Yet, like the cheeky rapscallion he used to be in his boyhood at Krishnanagar, he will time and again go against convention and play offbeat roles like that of an ageing author involved in an extra-marital affair in *Punascha* (2014). By and large, he has nevertheless accepted this new phase in his career with good grace. He cannot quit, and like the good foot soldier he continues to march on. It may not be artistically fulfilling to prop up mediocrity with undemanding but polished performances but it keeps him very busy, and he appreciates the virtues of being busy at this stage in his life. He chooses to not look back too much, lest he lose the strength to look forward again.

THEATRE: HIS ABIDING PASSION

Soumitra's devotion to the cause of theatre has been evident all through his career. He learnt the craft of acting from Sisir Bhaduri. He maintains that the solid foundation of everything he knows about acting precedes his cinematic debut. He rued not getting more time with the great actor. He began to go to him regularly after his theatre had closed down. He also acted with him once, when *Prafulla* was staged as a special show in 1957.

Soumitra has been both a panegyrist and defender of Sisir Bhaduri through his writings. In his collection of prose writings, a sizeable portion is devoted to his astute analysis of Sisir Bhaduri's contribution to the theatre as well as the genius of his craft. He watched his performances minutely and discussed theatre and acting at length. Sisir Kumar was a patient teacher and Soumitra absorbed everything that he could. In many ways, he considers himself his disciple and his manner of acting a reflection of his legacy.

His love for theatre and the stage had very deep roots. His first experience of acting was on the stages of Krishnanagar. When he moved to Calcutta it remained among his primary creative preoccupations. In Krishnanagar, he had first experienced the joys of enacting different characters, and how it could act as a kind of release from the shyness and uncertainties of boyish insecurities.

When he was in college in Calcutta, he acted in a play called *Mukhosh* which competed in the inter-university youth festival and won second prize. He and his friend Sushanto Bandyopadhyay were given the best actor award jointly.

When he eventually met Sisir Kumar, this passion turned into a vocation. It proved however to be a stepping stone because he shifted to cinema soon after. It has never been possible to have a well-balanced career straddling both the stage and the screen for too long. Besides, success in cinema came very early for Soumitra and it would have been rather easy to abandon the stage. It is therefore a testament to his great love for theatre that he tried his best to act in plays whenever he got the opportunity even in the heady first couple of decades of his career. He was in *Tapasi* (1963, directed by Debnarayan Gupta), *Sesh Raksha* (1965, directed by Anup Kumar), *Andha Yug* (1972, directed by Ajitesh Bandyopadhyay), *Krush-biddho Cuba* (1973, directed by Utpal Dutt), *20se June* (1975, directed by Jnanesh Mukhopadhyay).

This was not enough for him though. Sisir Kumar had asked him to translate Bertolt Brecht's *The Exception and the Rule*, and while his effort had not exactly thrilled his mentor, it did start off something in Soumitra. He has subsequently translated and staged several foreign language plays. In 1972, at the height of his career, he translated and staged Henrik Ibsen's *Ghosts* as *Bidehi* and in the very next year he translated and staged Clifford Odets's *The Big Knife* as *Rajkumar*. He acted in both of them and directed the productions as well. This was important to him in creative terms, but it was also significant for other reasons. His popularity as an actor ensured publicity for his projects and it benefitted the dwindling popularity of the Bengali theatre.

Not surprisingly, Ray praised the production values and the acting in these plays. He thought Soumitra's adaptations worked well. Soumitra remembers how he did not approve of his use of music in *Bidehi*. Ray advised him that music has to be used far more sparingly on the stage than in film, where its volume in conjunction with the spoken dialogue can be manipulated effectively. Soumitra had also developed a great love for western classical music. In his memoir he mentions how he had spent some time with Jyoti Basu, the Block Development Officer in Bardhaman and a western classical music aficionado. He played records for the curious actor and talked about the composers. When he told this to Ray, he compiled a list of classical pieces for him to listen to. He eventually listened to Ray, who after watching *Rajkumar* praised the acting and

The stage still has the capacity to challenge Soumitra
Photo courtesy of Pratap Dasgupta

adaptation but did not particularly like his use of western classical music. He curbed his use of background music thereafter, and he was happy to report that Ray never had reason to criticise the music in any of his subsequent theatrical adaptations.

These were however amateur efforts done mostly for Abhinetri Sangha. It was in 1978 that he turned professional with *Namjiban*. Interestingly, *Namjiban* was first adapted by his wife, Deepa Chatterjee, but it was never produced. Soumitra used her work for his first professional foray, tweaking it for his purposes. *Namjiban* earned both critical and commercial acclaim. In many ways, it was a crystallisation of long-cherished ideals and beliefs. He was the face of neo-realism in Bengali cinema, and he had imbibed its conventions and values. Heavily influenced by the sensibilities of Ray and the realism of Bansi Chandragupta's sets, Soumitra created a neo-realist template for Bengali theatre. In an interview with Shamik Bandyopadhyay, he recalled how Bansi used blowers to weather his sets in order to give it an authentic lived-in feeling. He used the same technique for the sets of *Namjiban* as well. It was unflinchingly realistic, eschewing all traditional conventions that would detract from it in any way. It so impressed Utpal Dutt that he wrote a long piece on it in his magazine *Epic Theatre*. He lauded Soumitra for his uncompromising idealism, and his refusal to indulge even the slightest bit of escapism. Soumitra who has always prided himself on being socially responsible and intellectually alert brought his convictions to the stage. The tenor of his artistic sensibilities always lay towards authenticity especially in the roles he portrayed. It ensured that there was always something relatable in the way in which he played his characters. It is hardly astonishing that his first professional play makes the 'audience face the harsh reality, and it questions the comfort zone of the petty bourgeoisie' (Utpal Dutt).

This was not the only time that he had incorporated cinematic techniques in his theatrical productions. In *Rajkumar* (1983), a play rife with metatextual reflections, he staged the life of an actor presented in subjective terms through the memory of the protagonist. He used images of himself from *Apur Sansar* and projected them on the background, a technique that is reminiscent of Tennessee Williams's use of cinematic devices to terrific effect in his plays. He understood the effectiveness of the visual image, and he played pivotal scenes in the play without dialogue. This emphasis on the visual element was something new in Bengali theatre. *Rajkumar* was however not a commercial success. It ran well for the first ten weeks or so after which collections dropped drastically. Soumitra reckons that the audience was not prepared to accept him in an avatar too far removed from his persona as a star in commercial cinema.

He bounced back quickly enough with *Nilkantha* (staged both in 1987 and 1997) which turned out to be both a critical and commercial success. His performance in *Nilkantha* is widely considered to be one of the finest dramatic performances in Bengali theatre. It was special too because his daughter, Poulami (who would go on to have a successful career on stage), acted with him. Perhaps the accolade he cherished most came from his mentor. Ray liked *Nilkantha* among all his plays the most and often referred to his performance in it as well-nigh unforgettable.

He followed up *Nilkantha* with *Ghatak Biday* in 1990, a comedy and a commercial smash that ran for more than 500 days. He was however more intellectually gratified with his previous plays. It was good fun to do a comic play, and there is much to be said for entertaining an audience. He had always balanced the demands of commercial cinema with his more serious interests, and it is not surprising that this should be replicated in his theatrical career as well. He had also adapted Anthony Shaffer's *Sleuth* (made into a film starring Laurence Olivier and Michael Caine in 1972 and again in 2007 with Michael Caine and Jude Law) into *Tiktiki* but that ran into its fair share of difficulties. He had originally envisioned himself as the young man and Utpal Dutt in the role immortalised by Laurence Olivier. This fell through and he approached Uttam Kumar, who not unpredictably wanted to make a film rather than commit to a play. The strangest part of all this was that there was no interest among producers to fund a project with two male leads and no female in the cast. He had to let the project slide until 1995, when he staged it with Kaushik Sen playing the younger character.

While it would be too much to say that Soumitra had a well-worked-out vision for Bengali theatre, it is true that he very intelligently played to his strengths both as an actor and as a director. His natural inclination towards realism determined his general approach. He says that at the beginning he did try to experiment with aspects of theatrical production. He did perhaps get carried away sometimes. In a conversation with Suresh Dutta, the person in charge of sets for *Namjiban*, he insisted on getting a brick wall made with plaster of paris. That was standard practice in film sets, and Soumitra was convinced that nothing else would give it that authentic look. Suresh pointed out that it would be impractical and dangerous to have a heavy wall that will need to go up and down several times. Soumitra remained unconvinced until Suresh offered to make it out of papier-mâché. He was not confident at all until he was given a sample of it made out of papier-mâché, at which point he admitted his mistake. It looked authentic enough, and he understood how very unfeasible his plan was.

He was far more intent on finding a middle ground that would allow him to seamlessly incorporate cinematic methods into existing theatrical traditions. Ever since cinematic acting developed according to the requirements of the form, there has been a gulf between the two modes of performance. Soumitra in an interview said that cinema gives an actor a lot of opportunities for very low-key, quiet and subdued acting. In fact, in most cases, it is actually better to underplay something because the camera can catch the slightest gesture and change in expression and magnify it tenfold. Acting in the theatre works on the principle of distance and therefore requires amplification of gesture, voice and expression for proper effect. Soumitra tried to tone down his performances on stage so that it can be as realistic as the circumstances would allow. He has written about the importance of being 'alive' on stage. It had to do with maintaining a consistent simulacrum of a real person on stage. He explained that in moments of passivity, when an actor does not have any dialogue, he should still try to maintain the illusion of verisimilitude with small gestures and general body language. Otherwise, the performance would go through phases of somnolence on stage.

Soumitra believes in the need to feel 'alive' on stage
Photo courtesy of Pratap Dasgupta

When he took on the role of Andrew Wyke in his adaptation of *Sleuth*, he was aware that he was playing an extremely idiosyncratic character. He had to add certain elements of eccentricities to his performances to effectively communicate the peculiarities of the character. Conversely, when he was performing in *Prantapasya* (1998), he felt that he had achieved a modicum of maturity in theatrical acting. He tried to do as less as possible and still convey the maximum amount of information to the audience. He abandoned all stylisation and concentrated on minimalist techniques. He made a conscious effort to make sure that he was always 'alive' on stage – whether it is through moving his hands in a particular way or through a distinct manner of looking at someone or something. Not uncharacteristically, while he was trying to minimise 'theatricality' in acting, he decided to try his hand at *jatra*, where the mode of acting is by necessity exaggerated and over the top. He did Utpal Ray's *Aamar Meye ke Phiriye Dao* in the mid 2000s, mostly because he had not done it before and wanted to try it out.

The gradual shift in sensibilities which we saw in his film career became apparent in theatre as well. In his earlier plays, he was expressing a more communal vision, of which he as an individual and performer was a part. It was consistent with a milieu in which he saw himself as a part of a coterie of artists who were working towards similar ends. Eventually, as he became the lone survivor of a bygone era, the plays become far more individualistic. His characters became embattled creatures, fighting for personal happiness in a hostile setting. Among the plays of this phase like *Homapakhi* (2006) and *Atmakatha* (2008), the most interesting is *Tritiyo Onko Otoeb* (2010). It was written and produced after he was diagnosed with cancer. It led to serious retrospection, coupled with fear and bouts of depression, which eventually led to this play. In it, three characters play the role of the actor in different phases of his life. It is searingly personal and confronts the prospect of death head on in a bid to accept it. Soumitra has never believed in autobiographies, and *Tritiyo Onko Otoeb* is the closest one can get to an individual statement about his own life. It is however a testament to the role art has played in his life. All through his career, he made the difficult choice of remaining truer to his passion as an artist than treat it as a conduit to fame and wealth. Even at this most difficult phase in his life, he tried to come to terms with the prospect of mortality through his art. He later recalled that people were not exactly comfortable with him talking about his own death in the play. He thought that acceptance can only come after it has been acknowledged without being in denial. His eventual message in the play was quite clear and it gives us an idea of his own attitude – do not allow the looming shadow of death to diminish all the joys of the time that is left. It is possible to be happy even with the awareness of the impending end. His enthusiasm for new projects and his undying ambition as an actor is a powerful reminder of how well he has internalised his own message.

Soumitra has written and spoken at length about theatre. He is candid enough about the shortcomings he sees in the system. One of his greatest performances was in Suman Mukhopadhyay's *Raja Lear* (2010), an adaptation of William Shakespeare's *King Lear*. Often considered to be one of the most difficult roles in theatre, Soumitra in spite of not having enough time for rehearsal put in a performance that received widespread acclaim. He played the role of the ageing patriarch whose tragedy was a brutally steep learning curve with great skill and passion. It is his most successful play, running to packed houses for its entire run. Yet, Soumitra's experience was far from happy. He later wrote bitterly about the attitude of the producers regarding remuneration. They did not talk about his payment until a day before the rehearsals were supposed to begin. He was committed by then, and felt slighted by the amount of money they were giving him. He points out that while this seems like an unduly mercenary attitude, it was the underhanded manner in which it was done that offended him. Soumitra's love for the stage can be gauged by his uncomplaining work in theatres that were subpar and from which he never did get a lot of money. He does not like being taken advantage of and, despite the plaudits, his memory of *Raja Lear* is somewhat tarnished by this. At other times, he has lamented the lack of discipline in theatres in Bengal. He recalls how a performance was thrown completely into pandemonium because a stray cat had wandered in during the show. There was chaos among the audience and the actors had to literally wait for the situation to return to normality. He does not take very kindly to crying infants either and wonders whether there is any point in bringing them for a live performance at all.

Whenever he is asked about the philosophy of his plays, he finds it difficult to give a straight answer. He is certain about the fact that his primary aim is to entertain the people. He started adapting western plays for Bengali audiences ever since Sisir Kumar gave him Brecht's play to translate. His rootedness in Bengali culture ensured the general approach and feel of all his subsequent adaptations. They never felt like western plays with Bengali dialogue, which would have clashed badly and would have seemed very out of context. Soumitra has a gift for changing the context and making it very regional and localised, so that it seems very relevant to his audience. It is this certainty about his own identity and artistic antecedents that allowed him to adapt according to the demands of the Bengali stage. This and his constant desire to incorporate newer techniques into theatrical productions will probably be his greatest legacy. His performances on stage (as in film) represent the best work done in Bengali theatre in the last few decades. As an octogenarian, his passion for theatre now outpaces his love of cinema. He is not as excited by what cinema has to offer him, but the stage still has the capacity to challenge him. While talking about the future, he invariably talks about the next production that he will be part of. His ambition as a performer now looks at the stage for inspiration, and as long as that is so, his artistic aspirations will remain intact.

RHYTHM AND HUES: POET AND PAINTER

The greatest of performers are quite often the most protective of their inner selves. Acting permitted Soumitra to be other people, which freed him up and allowed him to express an absolute profusion of moods, attitudes and personalities. He lived a great number of lives through his performances, but his most personal self has found expression in poetry and art.

Soumitra's poetry is a distillation of an idealistic sensitive soul
Photo courtesy of Pratap Dasgupta

In the Preface to his *Kabita Samagra* featuring his collection of poetry volumes, Soumitra writes that as far as he can remember, he did not start writing poetry under the influence of any ideology or a seminal influence. Like most sensitive young men, he first started writing poetry because he was infatuated with the idea of love. The first flush of love, the pangs of separation, and unrequited love found expression in his poetry. He would come back to these subjects again and again all through his poetry. Later, themes such as a yearning to return to nature, the need for a better society, and existential questions about life and death gradually found their way into his verses.

He recalls that it was really in his college days that the windows of his imagination opened up. He was introduced to the works of Jibanananda Das, Subhas Mukhopadhyay, Samar Sen and Buddhadeva Bose. In those days, one of his seniors had given him some sage advice that held him in good stead over the years. He had told Soumitra to not let a day pass by without writing something – 'not a day without a line'. This ensured a disciplined approach to writing poetry instead of waiting for inspiration to strike. The second piece of advice that Soumitra wisely embraced was that he should immediately forget what he writes so that he can write more. Consequently, he is not enamoured of his poetry and, in fact, cannot quote even a single one of them.

This particular attitude, moulded in his youth, made him reluctant to publish his poetry. Soumitra's friend the noted poet Shakti Chattopadhyay had once told him that if he publishes his poetry, he shall find it difficult to find new directions in his writings. However, it was eventually Shakti Chattopadhyay himself who one day brought along a publisher friend and stated that since the publishers were now seeking him out to publish his poetry, he should not turn them away. That was how his first volume of poetry came to be published. Among the many volumes of poetry that have been published, *Jalapropaater Dhaare Danrabo Bole*, *Baektigoto Nakshatramala*, *Shobdora Amaar Bagane*, and *Pore Achhe Chandaner Chita* are the most well received.

Poetry is inextricably bound with his childhood. His earliest memories are of his mother reading from Tagore's *Shishu* and *Shishu Bholanath* in her soft, dulcet tones. He fell in love with the rhythm of the poems that his mother

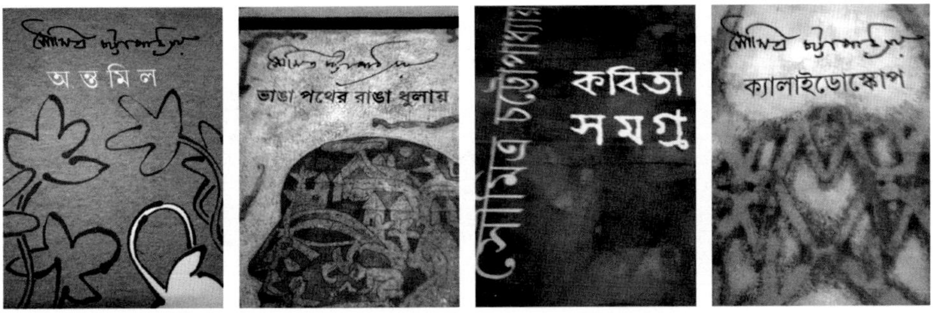

(Left to right) *Antameel*, *Bhanga Pather Ranga Dhulae*, *Kobita Samagra*, *Kaleidoscope* are among the many volumes of poetry by Soumitra that have been published over the years

read to him. Soumitra's grandfather Lalitkumar was himself a prolific writer. He had written Bagha Jatin's biography and young Pulu would read the book again and again, especially the part that narrated Bagha Jatin's hand-to-hand combat with a Royal Bengal tiger in the jungles of Koya. His father Mohitkumar's masterful rendition of Tagore's *Debotar Grash* overwhelmed a young Soumitra to the point where he lost sleep over it.

While the literary ambience at home nurtured a sensitive mind, Soumitra's experiences also moulded the budding poet in him. His idyllic surroundings in Krishnanagar, the vacations spent at Darjeeling, his firsthand experience of a communal riot in Howrah, and an encounter with the soldiers of the INA in Barasat, helped in the making of the man, and also the poet within.

As he grew to have a deeper and more passionate relationship with the written word, it slowly began to occupy a more private place as opposed to his more public career as an actor. Eventually it became associated with his closest thoughts unmediated through any other filter except his own consciousness. Acting was a collaborative art, and the value of a performance can often depend on a number of factors external to the actor himself. In its spontaneous flow and the absolute subjectivity of expression, poetry and art provide a unique insight into the man behind all those wonderful performances.

Soumitra is not entirely sure when he started writing poetry in earnest. What is not in any doubt is the overwhelmingly dominant influence of Rabindranath Tagore on his poetry. Tagore's poetry was part of the fabric of his family, and

Soumitra with poet Shankha Ghosh
Photo courtesy of Supriyo Nag

Soumitra reciting on stage
Photo courtesy of Pratap Dasgupta

became a naturally organic part of his sensibility when it eventually expressed itself in poetry. He was aware of this too and, in time, tried his best to find a voice of his own. It was not easy to break away from such an influence. However he knew that if he wished to forge an original voice, it would not do to slavishly imitate the great poet. As he grew older, the general direction of his intellectual growth that informed his decisions as an actor influenced him as a poet as well. His subjects were deeply personal, but they were not idiosyncratic and inaccessible. He found a way of translating the individual to something of larger significance. All through his career, Soumitra maintained that he did not believe in art that did not serve a greater social purpose. He followed this simple yet effective dictum in his poetry as well. There is a strong nostalgia that pervades his poetry, a desperate desire to go back to the winding Jalangi and the sun-kissed fields of Krishnanagar, where he romped in the delirious joy of childhood.

Crops are cradled in your arms
Why don't you drop some of them here
The sand vile sparkles in the sun
Crystal water beneath it

The crops are cradled in your arms
Don't lose them somewhere else
Let the weeds and wild ferns stay,

Crystal water flows beneath the sand here
Come and drop your crops here.

(*Tor kol bhora foshol*, 'Nostalgia', *Jalapropaater Dhaare Danrabo Bole*)

There are poems of angst in which the claustrophobic machinery of the city grates on his nerves and he contemplates all the things that have been sacrificed on the altar of empty materialism. There are echoes of an aching loneliness and the frustrations of being misunderstood that emerge from his poetry.

If I walk through this haze, I might reach near your loneliness someday, or I might never...
All those times that are lost between us, I search for in this mist...

(*Hoyto ei kuashar modhye diye hente gele...*, *Modhyanyo*, *Jalapropaater Dhaare Danrabo Bole*)

His strong political beliefs find expression in lines that are strident in their criticism and which call for a better society.

Come back fast to the wind
Does it have the bayonet in it?

Is the Santhal village shot yet?
Who all were they away from home that chilly night?
Can you recall? Can you remember that vacant village?
Being ransacked and searched by whose name?

The time piece glows through the night
The eyes and the teeth of the predator glisten
It glowed through the night,
The Poush *wind has a sharpness to it*
Each finger has an impatient trigger beneath it

If you've forgotten
Come back fast to the wind
The winter chill remembers it.

(*Phire Esho, Shobdora Amaar Bagane*)

On the other hand, there is a willingness to deal with the larger questions of life too. He talks about mortality and the finality of it; the need to look to one's children as a way to live on in a world of constant flux and change.

Thus as he laments the unforgiving passage of time and the uncertainties of life:
Will nothing at all be let off? The ungrateful years pass on, one after another,
Without even bothering to answer. Is this how you feel and love?
The winter wind shoves the queries aside and flees.
Your face turns dull, as I watch, your smirk tells me there's not much time left.

He then heaves a sigh of relief on seeing his young son:

And despite it all, time still totters in the mischief of our son.

(*Kichhui ki rehai pabe na, Mela e tar shonge*, *Jalapropaater Dhaare Danrabo Bole*)

It becomes the song of every ageing father whose fear of death is momentarily assuaged by the thought of his progeny carrying on even when he himself will not be around any more.

Soumitra's poetry is a distillation of an idealistic sensitive soul. He is forever caught between a desire to escape through memory to an idealised past and a need to engage with the troubles of reality. That is the base conflict in his poetry and provides much of its dramatic immediacy. The true surmise of Soumitra is in his poetry into which he pours his insights, doubts, consolations, admonitions and wisdom. His genius as a craftsman is evident in his career as an actor, yet the mind that informs those performances is best glimpsed through his poetry.

As I sit with my pen and notebook
The shackles around me break
And I can feel it
Then in the words I choose
This autumnal shedding ceases

With my pen and notebook
I can then pave a road
Where the breeze of freedom
Caresses me

Without my pen and paper
The economic needs dictate my ways
And dwarfed, I spend my days
With my pen and notebook

I can change this half rotten, putrid society
I can touch the sky then

I wouldn't know if it's known to others
My lungs are filled
With sands from this desert
The will-o-the-wisp that this sandy trail
Offers the thirst
With my pen and paper
I can reject them
And create a truthful, soothing oasis
One that will keep my path of deprivation canopied

With my pen and notebook
I can even
Once more
Give a shape to the love
That's disappeared long back
Like the burning camphor.

At a point of his poetic career, Soumitra felt that just writing poetry was not enough, and that there was also a need to create a literary platform for budding poets and writers. In 1961, along with Nirmalya Acharya, he came up with the literary magazine *Ekshan* so that they could publish their poetry independently as well as showcase other poets and writers. He remembers that there were no takers for their poetry then. Even though Soumitra was initially very reluctant, he agreed to jointly edit the magazine with Nirmalya Acharya after his wife Deepa intervened and convinced him to take joint responsibility. However, once he took the plunge he discharged his responsibilities as an editor in full earnest. Through the next decade he evolved as a person with a very fine editorial acumen.

Soumitra approached Satyajit Ray to suggest a name for his magazine. That is how the name 'Ekshan' came about. Ray designed the inaugural cover page and the logo for the magazine. He continued to illustrate the cover pages of all the issues until he became indisposed owing to his illness. Soumitra says Nirmalya Acharya and he would acquire material for *Ekshan* from different writers and poets introduced to them by their common friends at the Coffee House. After almost twenty years of co-editing the magazine, Soumitra decided to dissociate himself from *Ekshan* when he realised that as joint editors their wavelengths were not matching and their opinions differed in many ways. Nirmalya Acharya continued editing the magazine, and several of Ray's scripts were published in the magazine. In a time when a little magazine like *Krittibas* was paving the way for literary magazines, *Ekshan* carved out a niche for itself and even garnered critical acclaim from significant quarters.

Soumitra's art is even more private and personal than his poetry. He is the first to acknowledge that his dalliance with painting began as a way to while away the time. He never did like to waste any time, and painting was never meant to be a serious endeavour. Unlike his other artistic ventures, this one was undertaken without any real expectations. No one was more pleasantly surprised than him when he discovered that he had more than a little ability in this direction. He had always been a scholar of the visual arts, and long admired Ray's virtuosity. He admires the Surrealists very much, and singles out Van Gogh as his favourite painter. He marvels at his ability to imbue his landscapes with such a wide range of keenly felt emotions. When he was persuaded into holding an exhibition for his paintings, the critics too were quite taken by the strong originality of his artistic voice. His paintings are oddly beautiful and can be quite eerie too. They are nevertheless striking and speak of a vivid and bold personality.

Soumitra is entirely self-taught as an artist, even though he has been scribbling and doodling away for as long as he can remember. He had a couple of relatives, brothers with whom he was good friends, who were painters. He spent a fair bit of time with them in their youth. He learnt a few rudimentary techniques there too. When he was young, his uncle Somen Mukherjee's oil painting of St. Paul's cathedral left a lasting impact on his mind. In the late 1940s he used to visit his relative Chaitanyadeb Chattopadhyay, an accomplished master painter. A student of Abanindranath Tagore and therefore a follower of the Bengal School Movement, Chattopadhyay had his residence-cum-studio at Bhadrakali, Uttarpara. The young Soumitra admired the colours and compositions of the paintings at the studio. Years later Soumitra discovered a masterpiece by Chaitanyadeb Chattopadhyay on the first floor of the Academy of Fine Arts in Calcutta. It was a water colour composition depicting a group of people in various stages of bathing at the riverbank. Soumitra was amazed by the balance of the composition – thirty-nine human figures, each distinctly portrayed, and two ferry boats, yet nothing seemed cramped.

When Soumitra left his ancestral home in Krishnanagar and moved to Howrah, his neighbour turned out to be the renowned artist Rabin Mondol. He used to spend a lot of time at the artist's studio, watching him work. He would watch Mondol making sketches of Gandhiji while the Mahatma gave speeches at Howrah Maidan.

Young Pulu was introduced to many rare paintings through Bengali periodicals like *Bharatbarsha* and *Prabasi*. Works of Gaganendranath Tagore, Abanindranath Tagore, Nandalal Bose, Asit Haldar published in these periodicals captivated his impressionable young mind. Later, books on art further fuelled his interest. Satyajit Ray had gifted him a set of books on art on the occasion of his wedding. When Soumitra was felicitated on the completion of 100 days of one of his plays, he requested that instead of expensive gifts, he should be given books on art.

Soumitra readily admits that even when it came to art, it was Tagore who proved to have the greatest influence. It is more than probable that if he had pursued art with any seriousness, he would have been in the shadow of Tagore for years. He says that he has gotten rid of many paintings he has done over the years. He thinks that only a third probably has survived of his total output.

The informality of his doodling possibly took away the seriousness of it and he for a long while sketched and scribbled mostly for fun. He would sketch something on the back of cards and even add a couple of lines of his poetry to the image. He remembers giving these away to children and friends. He sketched voraciously in preparation for his plays and in preparation for his roles as well. Images of sets, costumes and even faces with the right make-up would accompany his notes on the production.

सत्य आर्ट गेलरी
cordially Invites you

An exhibition of Water Colours by

Shri. Soumitra Chatterjee
Actor, Recitator, Poet, Thespian

Opening: 5.00pm, Fri 8th Sep, 2017

Exhibition will be on display till
24th Sep, 2017 (12pm-9pm, Monday Closed)

Chief Guest
Shri Manu Parekh

Guest of Honour
Shri Jogen Chowdhury

Curated by
Shri Jyotirmoy Bhattacharya

Satya Art Gallery
Navajivan Trust
B/H Gujarat Vidyapith
Off Ashram Road, Navrangpura
Ahmedabad 380 014

Invitation card for an exhibition of Water Colours by Soumitra Chatterjee at Satya Art Gallery, Ahmedabad in 2017

Two water colour paintings by Soumitra exhibited at Satya Art Gallery, Ahmedabad in 2017
Photo courtesy of creativeyatra.com

Three water colour paintings by Soumitra exhibited at Satya Art Gallery, Ahmedabad in 2017
Photo courtesy of creativeyatra.com

His approach to painting does not have the same diligent preparation that goes into each role he essays whether in films or on the stage. In point of fact, he says that he searches more for a rhythm, waiting for faces half-hidden and tantalising in some obscure corners of his mind to emerge.

Soumitra seems to shy away from the subject of his paintings, while showing ready interest in discussing other painters. His great love for art is apparent in his tastefully furnished living room adorned with paintings, including that of eminent painter Rabin Mondol, who was also a close friend. As a matter of fact, he was persuaded into exhibiting his works by Rabin Mondol and Jogen Chowdhury who insisted that it deserves recognition. Soumitra took his time, since he was not keen on exhibiting his works. In 2013, a critically acclaimed exhibition of Soumitra's paintings titled 'Forms Within' was held at ICCR, Kolkata, attended by a host of celebrities as well as art connoisseurs. Renowned painter Wasim Kapoor was emphatic in his praise, when he expressed amazement at the quality of Soumitra's work. Kapoor stated that he is quite as good with a canvas as he has ever been in front of the camera. Another exhibition of water colours by Soumitra was held at Satya Art Gallery in Ahmedabad in 2017. Noted painter Jogen Chowdhury was the Guest of Honour at the exhibition in

Ahmedabad and he opined that, 'In his largely eventful life, the vast assortment of experience he has gathered, the keen assessments he has made, the varied characters he has portrayed and the different people he has encountered as part of his films and plays, find form and expression through his artwork. His paintings and sketches skilfully capture different facets of life; they are full of various little odd details that enhance their beauty.'

Soumitra however has a bit of a bemused smile when he talks about his art. He still does not really believe that it has got all the recognition it has, mostly because his somewhat playful attitude towards it has not changed much. Even though Soumitra refers to it as no more than *khela* (play), the accumulated experience of a life devoted to the arts nevertheless finds inventive ways to transform even the most absent-minded of efforts into something creative.

Soumitra's long life is a testimony of the worth of a life spent immersed in the creative arts, and to the value of an educated, cultured and sensitive soul dedicating itself to performance. He has played many roles on screen, and many in real life as well. He has been an inspiring and civilising presence in the realm of Bengali culture and one of its greatest ambassadors in the rest of the world. He lives modestly and yet harbours an ambition fiery enough to not be satisfied with his many accomplishments and rewards. He has spent his life reaching out for an artistic heaven that forever remains outside man's grasp. It is what drives him onward. He is one of the greatest actors this country has produced, and a fiercely intelligent man who has tried to live his life according to deeply cherished beliefs. His roles have become so integral to Bengali popular culture that each succeeding generation discovering him in awe will ensure his continuing vital presence in our consciousness. His greatest legacy is perhaps his continuing integrity and dedication as an artist in an industry that rarely acknowledges these virtues. A life lived on one's own terms is always the hardest, and its rewards if any may not always be adequate compensation. Soumitra admits that life has been hard at times, but he remains very grateful for the success and the love he has acquired over the many decades since he began his career. He hopes he has been deserving of all the adulation he has received. No one would ever doubt that he has deserved every last bit of it.

APPENDIX
READING HABITS OF SOUMITRA CHATTERJEE

The Books that shaped his Artistic Sensibilities

Lecture delivered in Bengali at a Sahitya Akademi programme in Calcutta on 6 November 1990

Neither a scholar nor a theoretician, I lack the benefit of a disciplined reader. Hence sowing the seed of the tree of knowledge in other people's minds is beyond both my ability and intentions. My journey through the land of books may as best be described as the joyride of an aimless wanderer.

My reading habits were always whimsical and undisciplined. And never was there any conscious effort on my part to preserve the essence of reading in the beehive of memory. Moreover, I have been engaged in such a profession during the last three decades where maintaining contact with recent publications is quite difficult. Entertaining people and reading books are inversely proportional with each other, I suppose.

During boyhood, the pleasure of reading was without any obligation, almost unreasonable. Now, necessity has become the mother of reading. Maybe I am playing a role where the age and background of the character I need to know. The concept of a role-to-be-acted remains incomplete without proper knowledge of the background of a character rooted in history or participating in a social upheaval. It goes without saying, however, that the roles of most of the Bengali movies of today do not usually make such demands on an actor. But in theatre, especially in adaptation of a foreign play, one has to search for an objective correlative in one's native land for absorbing the dimensions of the alien character. For example, once we were adapting a European play based on Thirty Years' War or War of the Roses, where the warring groups, though belonging to the same religion, were two hardcore sects viz. Roman Catholic and Protestant. For giving the adaptation an Indian flavour, it was necessary to know if our history offers any such parallel. It was necessary to know how organised were fighting armies then, how the hierarchical arrangement was from the highest general down to the ordinary soldier, their respective salaries, work allotment, uniforms, weapons, what was the method of recruitment, arrangement of cooking, etc. Above all, it was necessary to learn of the then condition of the common man, the availability and price of food-stuffs and clothes, and the system of currency. With these aspects in mind, I began the search and found the desired parallel in the *Fall of the Mughal Empire* by Sir Jadunath Sarkar, which describes the clash of the two Muslim sects – Shia and Sunni – during the decadence of the Mughal Age. This book in four volumes records almost in a daily diary form important information about our political, social and economic history of the time. Another book of Sir Jadunath entitled *Army of the Indian Mughal* supplied me with all the details about the then army organisation that I was looking for. Thus reading now is a pleasure not without profit.

From a native mofussil town we often came to visit our relatives in Calcutta. A naughty child as I was, my elders considered me a bother. I am told that the best remedy to still me was to sit me down with a book. The home of my paternal aunt boasted a very big library built up by Sir Ashutosh Mukhopadhyay and later handed over to the National Library. Sir Ashutosh was my aunt's father-in-law. The huge racks of his library were the favourite hide-and-seek spot for us, the children of the family. I still wonder how, in course of the game, I would often be separated from the group and would start browsing over the books. I could hardly make out the meaning of many of them. But my tender soul would seek unknown mystery in their illustrations and words. I still remember thumbing over the *Arabian Nights*, *Robinson Crusoe*, *Book of Knowledge* and such other books in that library first. The tales of the *Arabian Nights* would transport me on the wings of imagination. Exotic names of people and places, their customs, garments – all these topical allusions would reconstruct in my mind the life of the unknown people of the unknown land. Day after day my mind would wander on the island of Robinson Crusoe. An idle sorrow, an unreasonable anguish would fill my mind – where are these lands? How does one reach there? The physical journey was substituted by the flying saucer of books.

The library in my aunt's house had more books in English than in Bengali. There were, of course, many Sanskrit titles. But these titles in the language of the gods used to scare me like Sir Ashutosh's books on Arithmetics. In school, Arithmetics and Sanskrit were always my Waterloo. Hence, one cultivated a safe habit of revering these books from a long distance. However, by virtue of being a student of Bengali language and literature during the university days, some informal friendship could be struck with a few Sanskrit books. With handy reference to Bengali and English translations, I tried to study at this stage books like Kalidasa's *Meghadut*, *Abhijnan Sakuntala*, *Kumar Sambhava*, Jayadev's *Gitagovinda* and Sanatan Goswami's *Ujjval Nilamani*.

There was, however, God's plenty of Bengali books in my maternal aunt's house. The patriarch of this family, a maternal grandfather of mine, was Sourindramohan Mukhopadhyay, a famous Bengali novelist. Along with vast accumulation of world literature, his home was a favourite meeting place of the litterateurs. He wrote a number of books for children. He gave me full freedom to roam at will amidst his collections. Not being endowed with a very good memory, I cannot recollect the titles which I read there. What is still distinctly imprinted on my mind is the refined and cultured atmosphere of Sourindramohan's home. Moreover, to see a flesh-and-blood writer penning his books just in front of you was definitely awe-inspiring enough to urge a young soul to love books and the world of books all the more.

My own paternal grandfather, an advocate in Krishnanagar, was also a writer of novels, travelogues, biographies, memoirs, etc. Two of his books drew me much; one, an intimate biography of Jatindranath Mukhopadhyay, the great Bengal revolutionary, who was a childhood friend of grandpa and with whom he even served a prison term as an activist; the other, a booklet recording affectionate memoirs of the annual Durgapuja festival held at our ancestral village Koya near Selaidaha. The picture of the village life in the early 20th century Bengal drawn in this booklet fascinated me. Moreover, intricate family history recorded in the book by grandpa imbibed in me a deep sense of tradition and a spirit of patriotism.

The drawing room was packed with grandpa's law books. But an inner chamber, usually called 'reading room', was lined with almirahs full of other books. My parents also loved books and those were family collections, some won by my parents as prizes in recitation competitions, etc. Issues of many magazines and journals, bound annually, also found place there. These included the famous *Prabasi* and *Bangadarshan* and also juvenile magazines like *Mouchak*, *Sandesh*, etc. It is from these almirahs that I first read Lamb's *Tales from Shakespeare*, Stevenson's *Treasure Island*, *Dr Jekyll and Mr Hyde*, Scott's *Ivanhoe*, Harriet Stowe's *Uncle Tom's Cabin* and even Tolstoy's *Resurrection*. It goes without saying that fully appreciating the content of these books was beyond my scope at that young age. Still, a dumb and atavistic hunger urged me to read on.

Arthur Conan Doyle's Sherlock Holmes stories used to charm my mind with the intoxication of mystery and romance. I enjoyed reading these stories at later stages also. Maybe then the appeal was more cerebral – of the writer's innovative use of language and subtle intelligent manipulation of plot. Among the other stories of adventure, travel and hunting that I read, Jim Corbett was predominant. To his *Man Eaters of Kumaon*, *Temple Tiger*, *Jungle Lore* and also *My India*, I came back again and again. Not just for the euphoric excitement of hunting, nor merely for the beautiful language and engaging style of story-telling, nor only for the environmental appeal of the vast virgin Nature, but for the delectable portraits of the apparently non-descript day-to-day life of the common man of India which are almost without parallel. The poor helpless forest-dwellers come alive in the pages of these stories with their courage, honesty, hospitality, capability of sacrifice and above all strength of character. My heart bows down in reverence to this white-skinned hunter when I find these stories replete with love and compassion for Mother India and her people.

During my growth from childhood to boyhood, a few more books left deep imprint on my mind. Two of them were Eric Maria Remarque's *All Quiet on the Western Front* and James Jean's *Mysterious Universe*. I read them in Bengali translation. About the same time, I started reading Bibhutibhushan Bandyopadhyay's *Pather Panchali*. There was hardly anyone in our generation who has not identified with Apu of *Pather Panchali*. Many of us mentally walked down the highway of larger life that Apu took from Nischindipur via Calcutta. Even in a literal sense, many of us found ourselves transported from village to town almost in an identical fashion. How would I know at the time of reading *Pather Panchali* that my acting career would also cross its adolescence through acting in the role of Apu in future?

From the family collection my further reading consisted of a series of novels of Bankimchandra published by the Basumati Sahitya Mandir. That probably marked the beginning of my foray in Bengali fiction. The beginning was an inch away from the graph, as most of the boys in our time were initiated in the world of Bengali fiction through Saratchandra. Even today, therefore, if anyone expresses his dislike for Bankim's novels, I feel scandalised. After *Ananda Math*, much has been said about Bankim, the seer (Rishi), the inspired creator of the hymn *Bandemataram*, the champion of Indian nationalism. Accusing fingers have been raised against him for what many term as his pro-British and anti-Muslim tendencies. Such criticism leaves me cold. I wonder if someone hails the British as good rulers against the backdrop of extreme anarchy and misrule in the wake of a decadent Moghul Empire or if he views the British as purveyor of a Progressive European culture, then could his thoughts be called unjust, irrespective of whether they are right or wrong? Then again to avoid proscription of books many writers of the time utilised the Muslim rulers as dummy characters for their British prototypes. Hence, it is unwise to reach a hasty conclusion that Bankim had an ingrained hatred for the Muslims. On the contrary, many passages may be cited from his writings to show his respect and love for them. Above all, whatever may yield by the subtle, socio-political analysis, how can one ever deny the greatness of Bankim as a novelist? Had he not unlocked the doors of boundless possibilities for Bengali prose, surely Rabindranath would not have been able to elevate it later to the higher level of world literature.

In the rickety libraries of the mofussil towns of Bengal, apart from Bankim, Rabindranath and Saratchandra's books, one could lay hands on Sasadhar Datta's adventure series of Dacoit Mohan, biographies suitable for younger readers published by Deva Sahitya Kutir and abridged Bengali translations of Victor Hugo, Charles Dickens, Alexander Dumas and such other continental writers. My gluttony for reading would take in all these. In our times, most of the guardians discountenanced such reading habits. Any book outside the school syllabus was called a 'story book'. There used to be a rapid reader in English and Bengali courses of the school in those days. In a relatively higher class when I found a 'story book' like *David Copperfield* as a rapid reader in the syllabus, I felt the drudgery of preparing school lessons was, as if, slightly mitigated.

On being promoted to a higher class, we were not necessarily rewarded with new books. Most of the books had to be bought secondhand from an erstwhile student of that class at half price. Hence, whenever a revised syllabus was introduced, our joy knew no bounds. For, the guardians now would be compelled to buy us crisp and print-smelling new books. My plight was bad as such. Along with the shirts and shoes I had to usually inherit the books of my elder brother. In the matter of 'story books', however, there was no question of inheriting. It was always a case of joint ownership. Thus *Sishu*, *Mukut*, *Thakurmar Jhuli* and such other titles were jointly owned by myself and my elder brother.

Our childhood companions like Abanindranath Tagore's *Rajkahini*, Upendrakishore Roychoudhuri's *Tuntunir Boi* or Sukumar Ray's *Abol Tabol* came back to me by the inevitable law of the cyclic order, when my children started growing up. To satisfy their demand for tales, I had to refresh my memory. In the process I discovered that the two decades which passed in between have changed certain things. Urbanisation and industrial development have beaten back the folk-etymology and folk-culture of Bengal. It was never necessary to explain to us what was meant by a *jola* (weaver) or *malo* (fisherman). These classes of people were around us. Now, they are gone much farther away from the young ones of the 'genteel' families.

The two epic tales of India that transcended time reached me through Upendrakishore Roychoudhuri's *Chhotoder Ramayan* and *Chhotoder Mahabharat*. At a more mature stage, I studied the Bengali translations of Rajsekhar Basu and Kaliprasanna Sinha. Like most of my fellow-countrymen, *Ramayan* and *Mahabharat* have become a part of my inner consciousness too. I am also a beneficiary of the delight and inspiration that these two epics have supplied to crores of people by their radiant heroism, colourful characterisation, flights of poetry and philosophical enlightenment. As documents of lost social history and reflection of by-gone values also these epics have always supplied food for thought. Though the characters in the *Ramayan* and *Mahabharat* are portrayed larger than life, it is among common people around us that I have noticed the dichotomy of Ramchandra, justness of Yudishthira, genius of Arjuna and greatness of Karna. It is among the frail women around me that I have seen the sorrow of a Sita, unbiased humanitarianism of a Gandhari or the fiery brilliance of a Panchali. I have never conceived them as gods or goddesses of Hindu pantheon fossilised by custom or ritual. It is with the heroism, weakness, instinct and greatness of the humankind that they have enriched my mind.

Imprint of the variety of human life notwithstanding, reasoned thinking never suggests that characters like Rama or Ravana, Bhima or Ghatotkacha, Krishna or Putana ever existed historically or even in prehistoric age. If the hero of an epic is to be considered a historical character, then the various fantastic incidents described in the epic need also to be accepted as true and plausible. In that case, one cannot doubt that there were flying chariots; or that mother's womb was not absolutely necessary for one's birth, one might emerge from the furrow at will. If one is ready to accept as historical events such phenomena as Ram-devotee Hanuman's crossing the sea in one long-jump, preventing daybreak by obliterating the Sun in his armpit or wilfully enlarging his body to the measure of a mountain, only then one is entitled to assert Ram's historical existence also. Moreover, to conclude that Ram existed, one has to reach another corollary-conclusion that the imagination of Valmiki, the greatest poet of our land, was so poor and shallow that he needed the physical presence of a man to model his epic on. And *Ramayan* then becomes nothing but a documentary of the life of a man called Ram.

Not only *Mahabharat*, even *Ramayan* does not seem to have been written by one poet. In the first canto of Adiparva, the narrator (*pathak*) Souti says "Some poets have sung this history earlier, now others are singing, again in future still others will sing." The illuminating analysis of 'Jay-Vijay', the source and core-book of the *Mahabharat* made by Iravati Karve in *Yugant* further confirms this belief. Generations of poets at various times have incorporated the experiences of their life, their ideals and imagination into the existing myth and legend and thus helped convert the saplings of Valmiki and Vyasa into big banyan trees. On that score, *Ramayan* and *Mahabharat* are not creations of individuals, but of the society. Hence, not one Ram or one Yudhishthir, but many Rams and Yudhishthirs conglomerated together to make up the heroes of these epics.

Thus the history recorded in the *Ramayan* and *Mahabharat* is not of an individual, but of the society. If one has to search for history in these epics, one has to tear the curtain of allegory and seek the Truth inside. Is it impossible that Draupadi's polygamy reflects the matriarchal society of the Pratnayuga? Will it be wrong to interpret the allegory of the burning of Khandav as the ruthless Aryan expedition to convert the forest into human habitats in the wake of agrarian civilisation? Can it be much remote from truth if one thinks that those who died by the arrows of Arjuna and the disc of Krishna while trying to flee from the devastating forest fire were not just dreadful beasts, but the primitive tribes of this subcontinent who had snakes, birds, etc., as their totem? Will it be a great mistake to consider Moydanav, the Visvakarma of the demons, whose life Krishna saved at the behest of Arjuna, and whose great architectural genius was later displayed in building the magnificent Pandava capital Indraprastha, as the representative of the primitive Indian civilisation that flourished in Mohenjodaro and Harappa much before the advent of the Aryans?

Bankimchandra once lamented, "The people of this wretched country believe that whatever is there in *punthi*s (ancient manuscripts) must have been said by sages and hence Absolute Truth." If one concludes from the *punthi*s that the amphibian chariot Pushpak was a reality, one would be wandering in the mist of unscientific confusion. But does it diminish the glory of the epic if one thinks that the poetic fancy perceived the human quest for aerial flight and previewed the aeroplane in Pushpak? Shaking off the opium of devotion, can't we make sincere attempts to understand these epics in the light of reason, from sociological standpoint with the aid of his story, anthropology and such other disciplines? The kind of attempts made by George Thomson in the book *Aeschylus and Athens*?

There was not much religious orthodoxy in the middle class Hindu family in which I was brought up. We were taught to respect other religions also. Still, it is my reading habits that really helped me get rid of religious superstitions altogether. From the very boyhood, Tagore's writings became my staple readers. The more I advanced in Tagore studies, the more shattered were conservative, narrow religious and social prejudices in my mind. Another factor also helped me achieve this. My reaching the stage of adolescence coincided with permanently migrating to the great city of Calcutta from the small mofussil town. This city of Rabindranath, Michael, Vidyasagar, Vivekananda and Subhashchandra as if pushed my mind perforce towards the greater World. For quite some time, I stayed very near College Street, the book bazaar of Calcutta. Almost automatically the habit grew of browsing over ancient books from the railing of Presidency College as well as of buying books through petty savings of pocket money.

During my college education at Calcutta, I came across many erudite teachers and knowledgeable friends. I was a student of Professor Narayan Gangopadhyay, a famous fictionist of Bengal. His legendary lectures and presentations in the classroom effortlessly inculcated a love for literature in the mind of the students. It is about this time that I was acquainted with Gourmohan Mukhopadhyay, a passionate reader, who inspired us to dive deeper into serious literature. With him I spent hours in the National Library, University Library, Brahmo Samaj Library and such other places. I switched over to Arts during my graduation, after studying Sciences for two years. Hence most of my studies at that stage were literature-centric, not just creative literature, but also literary criticism, history of literature, poetics, aesthetics and such other subjects.

It is Gourmohan who introduced me to the Calcutta Theatre circle. Both of us were spell-bound by the legendary histrionic talent of Sisirkumar Bhaduri. The image of the great actor in our mind was further brightened by the fame of his learning. During my post-graduation, I got an opportunity to know Sisirkumar personally. The tentative acquaintance gradually developed into an intimate relationship. And one important common factor responsible for this was love of books. His vast personal library had by then thinned down to around 2,000 books only due to repeated shifting of residence and inconvenience of preservation facilities. Once he commented, 'How I feel like revising the books read in early life. Can you fetch me some such books?' From then onwards, it was a regular routine for me to carry a few books to his residence every weekend and borrow one from his collection, as if by exchange. Next week our conversation would invariably begin with the books we read. He possessed a kind of literary conscience that brightened any discourse. I distinctly remember that the last book which I supplied to him before his death was E.K. Chamber's two-volume *Medieval Stage*.

Once I had the rare opportunity to share the stage with Sisirkumar. On the eve of the rehearsal he told me, 'First read the drama thoroughly. Read like a detective. Just as a detective reconstructs the whole incident from tell-tale clues, similarly try to find out whatever meaning is there hidden behind the dialogue.' Till today, I consider this sharp inquisitive study a must for an actor.

Next day, I received at home an altogether unexpected honorarium for my performance. That was my first income as an actor. I spent the amount in buying a few books as gift for Sisirkumar. One of the books was Jibanananda Das's *Rupasi Bangla*, my all-time favourite. Sisirkumar was not much of a reader of modern Bengali poetry. But when he turned the pages and recited in his inimitable voice the short introductory verse, the poem came alive. Then he said in a distant tone of sorrow, 'This *chalta*-blossom, song of the owl for the goddess Lakshmi, calm lamp, smell of the soggy earth, faint murmur – will these really survive forever? Where is that glorious Bengal and where are those Bengalis?'

Though not conversant with modern Bengali poetry, Sisirkumar was well-versed in modern world theatre. He introduced me to the writings of Brecht in the fifties when hardly anyone in Bengali theatre was acquainted with the name, what to speak of studying him. It is he who in 1957 egged me on to adapt into Bengali Brecht's *The Exception and the Rule*. Gradually, under the tutelage of Sisirkumar, the desire to become a full-fledged actor started crystallising in my mind. Hence my studies were also converging to plays, dramaturgy, theatre, art of acting, etc. Marlowe, Shakespeare, Ben Jonson, Moliere, Arthur Miller, Tennessee Williams, Materlink, Michael Madhusudan Dutt, Dinabandhu Mitra, Girishchandra Ghosh, Dwijendralal Roy, et at kept me busy. Perhaps Aristotle's *Poetics* or Allardyce

Nicoll's *Theory of Drama* are no longer considered infallible yardsticks of dramatic judgement, but it is these books from which I gathered preliminary knowledge of dramatic theme, composition, style, structure, characterisation, etc. No longer do I believe in such Aristotelian rigidities that there cannot be any tragedy without awe and grandeur arising out of the fall of the great, or that the aim of the tragedy is catharsis or purification of the spectators' mind through pity and terror or that there must be unity of time, place and action in a drama. But that conflict is the soul of a drama or that in creating the illusion of reality, probable impossibility is more effective than improbable possibility – these I believe to be true still today.

Around this time, A.C. Bradley's *Shakespearean Tragedy* and *Oxford Lectures on Poetry* helped me much in realising the nature of tragedy as well as drama in general. Also I found a bright example of what Sisirkumar termed as 'detective interest' in Dover Wilson's *What Happened in Hamlet*.

Like all other serious actors, I was greatly influenced by Stanislavsky's *My Life in Art*. Whatever tips I got from this book about the art and technique of acting are still relevant to me. At a later stage, I got acquainted with Brecht's alienation theory. But now in these advancing years, I have realised that it is the Stanislavskian identification which is the basic pre-requisite for a good actor. Even, a sort of integration of both identification and alienation seem achievable now. Being supplementary to each other, these two methods may invest the actor with the desirable dialectics between optimum identification and optimum alienation. I should also like to mention a lesser known book that I read during my youth. The title is *On Actors and True Art of Acting*, written by George Henry Lewis, husband of the famous Victorian novelist Mary Ann alias George Eliot. Lewis was not just an actor and playwright. He wrote extensively on this art; the depth and insight of these writings fascinated me at that time and still do.

Side by side with studies in theatre, my wandering among books in general was continuing at random. About this time, I spent days and nights together in a kind of daze on reading Romain Rolland's *Jean Christophe*. 'Go on to Death, you who must die! Go and suffer, you who must suffer! You do not live to be happy ...Suffer, die. But be what you must be – a Man!' Such lines still rejuvenate the inspiration of my youthful days. Christopher's words to Otto, 'Money – I hate the word and the thing itself," sounded to me like an indignant protest against the consumerism of the capitalist world. In those days, I was inspired by reading the story of the scientists' crusade against bacteria in *Microbe Hunters*. Such books as Gorky's *Mother*, Fuchike's *Notes from the Gallows* or Nikolai Astrovosky's *How the Steel was Tempered* reaffirmed my faith in man's capacity to struggle and to build up resistance.

Anyway, I suppose it is both pointless and unnecessary to mention individual books in this way. As a matter of fact, it is the accumulated effect of reading hundreds of such poems, stories, plays and histories that gradually builds up into an optimistic realisation of the depth of human life. Let me rather conclude this talk by referring to two such books which helped me in forming a well-defined approach towards mankind, society and history.

As I have mentioned earlier, my crossing over to youth coincided with coming over to Calcutta. Here was a different atmosphere of political intensity. Hence, as a college student, I also got entangled with students' movement and its concomitant politics. During my childhood days, our home basked in the sun of Independence struggle. Both my father and grandfather served prison terms during Swadeshi movement. I was thus emotionally involved with the dream of freedom. But the change of rulers in 1947 could not bring about much liberation in the life of the common people. When the sensitive mind of my early youth was easily moved and angered by the suffering of the toiling masses of my country, I was inevitably drawn towards a few books of Marx and Engels. First among these was *Communist Manifesto*, the very opening sentence of which enunciated an epochmaking thought about the history of human civilisation, "The history of all hitherto existing society is the history of class struggles." None has looked at history from this angle earlier. It is this book which gradually made me realise that " . . . oppressor and oppressed, stood in constant opposition to one another, carried on an uninterrupted, now hidden, now open fight, a fight that each time ended, either in a revolutionary re-constitution of society at large, or in the common ruin of the contending classes. . .The modern bourgeois society that has sprouted from the ruins of feudal society has not done away with class antagonisms. It has but established new classes, new conditions of oppression, new forms of struggle in place of the old ones. Our epoch, the epoch of the bourgeoisie, possesses, however, this distinctive feature: it has simplified the class antagonisms. Society as a whole is more and more splitting up into two great hostile camps, into two great classes directly facing each other: Bourgeoisie and Proletariat.'

There may be a lot of debate on how far has Marx's prophecy proved true or false, but to me this new interpretation of human history has remained as incontrovertible as it was in those days. But today even those countries which witnessed socialistic revolution through applied Marxism are now looking for new state structure discarding Marxism. Does this change mark further human progress and emancipation from shackle? Perhaps the answer still lies in the womb of future. Whether these countries ultimately turned out to be 'established new classes, new conditions of oppression' – these doubts also cannot be totally solved by contemporary judgement. But the light that Marx and Engels focused on many hitherto unexplored truths about human life and society would remain as brilliant as ever. Unwavered will remain the truth of these much-quoted lines: 'In the social production of their means of existence men enter into definite necessary relations which are independent of their will, productive relationships which correspond to a definite stage of development of their material productive forces. The aggregate of these productive relationships constitutes the economic structure of the society, the real basis on which a judicial and political superstructure arises, and to which definite forms of social consciousness correspond. The mode of production of the material means of existence conditions the whole process of social, political and intellectual life. It is not the consciousness of men that determines their existence, but, on the contrary, it is their social existence that determines their consciousness.'

As I read the Marxian analysis in such books as Christopher Caudwell's *Illusion and Reality* and *Studies in a Dying Culture*, George Thomson's *Aeschylus and Athens*, Ralph Fox's *Novel and the People*, Erewest Fisher's *Necessity of Art*, I was more and more convinced that the form and content of literature are always determined by the social, economic and historical aspects of human civilisation.

Mutability is the law of life. There will be changes in our approach to Marx and Engels. New generations will assess in the light of changed realities the philosophical concepts of Marxian dialectics. But there can never be a denial of the fact that these leaders of speculative thought supplied the weapon of confidence to the oppressed proletariats in their struggle for liberation. Many a time when I was plunged in despair at the cruelty, unscrupulousness, anarchy and hypocrisy of this decadent society, it was the prop on Marxist philosophy that helped me comprehend the situation and sustain my faith in future.

Thus it is that books have played an all-powerful moderator's role in my life. At times when morning blues would induce seminal questions like 'What is life?' 'What shall I do with this life?' it is from the pages of books that answers flash themselves. At the hour of love, book was there as the sportive, wanton maiden-attendant. At the time of unmitigated sorrow, book was there as the consolatory balm. At the time of utter loneliness, book gave the company of a close friend. And at the time of fierce struggle, book acted as the instrument of work and weapon of battle. It is the books that tied me in an inseparable knot with fellowman, with life.

Translated from Bengali by Nirmal Kanti Bhattacharjee

LIST OF REFERENCES

Chatterjee, Soumitra. 2014. *The Master and I*. New Delhi: Supernova Publishers.

Chattopadhyay, Soumitra. 2016. *Gadya Sangraha: Collection of Essays by Soumitra Chattopadhyay* vols 1 and 2. Kolkata: Dey's Publishing.

Gooptu, Sharmistha. 2010. *Bengali Cinema: An Other Nation.* New Delhi: Roli Books.

Kael, Pauline. 1977. "Lost and Found". In *Reeling*. Little Brown.

Majumdar, Boria. 2016. *Feluda @ 50*. HarperCollins Publishers India.

Nag, Amitava. 2016. *Beyond Apu: 20 Favourite Film Roles of Soumitra Chatterjee.* HarperCollins Publishers India.

Nandy, Pritish, and Tapan Chaki, ed. 2019. *Peerless Minds: An Arc of Achievement.* HarperCollins Publishers India.

At the editorial desk of *Ekshan*. Photo by Mona Choudhury
Photo courtesy of Debasish Mukhopadhyay